How to
REACH YOUR
FULL POTENTIAL
for GOD

How to
REACH YOUR
FULL POTENTIAL
for GOD

Charles F. Stanley

THOMAS NELSON
Since 1798

NASHVILLE   DALLAS   MEXICO CITY   RIO DE JANEIRO

Published in Nashville, Tennessee, by Thomas Nelson. Thomas Nelson is a registered trademark of Thomas Nelson, Inc.

Thomas Nelson, Inc., titles may be purchased in bulk for educational, business, fund-raising, or sales promotional use. For information, please e-mail SpecialMarkets@ ThomasNelson.com.

Unless otherwise noted, Scripture quotations are taken from THE NEW KING JAMES VERSION. © 1982 by Thomas Nelson, Inc. Used by permission. All rights reserved.

Library of Congress Cataloging-in-Publication Data

Stanley, Charles F.
  How to reach your full potential for God : what you must learn from the bold confrontations of Christ / Charles F. Stanley.
      p. cm.
    ISBN 978-1-4002-0092-4
    1. Self realization—Religious aspects—Christianity. 2. Christian life—Baptist authors. I. Title.
BV4598.2.S73 2009
248.4—dc22   2009024964

Printed in the United States of America

10 11 12 13 WC 5

CONTENTS

To Rebecca, my mother, who challenged me early
in life to reach my full potential.

CHAPTER 1

DO YOU WANT GOD'S BEST?

I awoke suddenly one morning about three o'clock. I had been soundly and deeply asleep. But in an instant, I was sitting up in my bed wide awake with this question burning in my spirit:

Do you want to reach your full potential?

I have experienced similar encounters in the past and have come to recognize that when something like this happens, God is trying to get my attention. More importantly, He is about to impart to me something I need to know or something I need to preach.

Immediately I replied, "Yes, Lord!"

I didn't hesitate or ponder the question. Without a doubt I want to be and to do all that God has created me to be and to do! That is my deepest heart's desire.

I reached for the pad of paper and pencil that I keep by my bedside for just such words from the Lord, switched on the light, and began to write as He spoke into my spirit. *If you truly want to reach your full potential, you must have a clean heart, a clear mind, a balanced schedule.* Within a matter of minutes, I had completely outlined the content of the book you are holding in your hands.

Then I turned off the light and fell back into a sound, restful sleep knowing that I had heard directly from God.

When morning came, I got down on my knees and prayed about the words that the Lord had given me during the night. I knew with certainty that I was to preach His message—a message not only for me, but also for the entire body of Christ.

I could hardly wait for Sunday to arrive so I could launch into this wonderfully rich area of the Father's concern—reaching *your* God-given potential.

The truth is, many people are not pursuing their potential. They are not factoring God into their decision-making or into their goal setting. They cannot clearly and succinctly say what they believe to be the Lord's foremost purpose and plan for their lives. They will stare at you blankly if you ask, "What do you believe is God's will for you? Why do you believe He created you? What is the Father leading you to do next in your life?"

Let me assure you at this book's outset of several great truths:

First, God has a will, plan, and purpose for your life individually and personally. He has a broad will, plan, and purpose for all of mankind, and He has specifically designed you and equipped you to fulfill a portion of that bigger will, plan, and purpose. You are not here by accident. You are not on this earth merely to live a certain number of years, months, and days, and then die. You are here to accomplish a job that God assigned to you from eternity past.

Second, your heavenly Father has already embedded into you all of the gifts and talents you need to complete the work that He has assigned, prepared, and provided for you to do. God has already embedded into you all of the raw material necessary for you to come into a relationship with Him and to develop the character of His Son, Jesus Christ. Your job is to discover the talents that God has placed in you, to develop them, and to begin to use them as the Lord brings opportunities for service or ministry.

Third, nobody can be who you are, nobody can replace you, and nobody else on this earth is capable of fulfilling the Father's plan for you. Nobody else can do the work He has gifted you to do, know the people He is leading you to know, or offer the praise and prayer that He is giving voice to. You must be and do what God made you to be and do.

Fourth, you must establish firm commitments in various areas of your life in order to pursue and begin to reach your God-given potential. It doesn't unfold accidentally or automatically. The pursuit of your unique potential and purpose requires you to seek God's very specific help in very specific areas of your life.

The question I ask you at the outset of this book is the same question the Lord asked me:

"Do *you* want to reach *your* full potential?"

If your answer is yes, then this is His message for you.

CHAPTER 2

DON'T SETTLE FOR LESS

Are you excited about your life?

Or do you feel as if you are merely existing?

Are you moving with confidence toward a desired goal?

Or do you feel as if you are drifting along from day to day without any sense of purpose or direction?

Perhaps there was a time when you were excited about your life, but now the excitement has faded, and you are asking, *What has happened to me? Why am I so apathetic about my life? What happened to my inner drive?*

People have said to me, "When I look at my life and the way the world is today, I just don't see much to be excited about."

Some think about their vocations or jobs and say, "I can't go any higher, do any better, or go any farther. I can't do more than I'm doing right now."

Others feel as if their lives have gone stale. Perhaps their marriages aren't as dynamic as they once were, or they have lost all interest in hobbies and activities that once gave them pleasure.

Some people tell me that they feel inadequate or unprepared for the future.

Still others say that they feel plagued by their lives—stuck in their circumstances, wondering, *What's it all about? What is my life worth? What happened to my joy?*

There are reasons we feel stuck, discouraged, or adrift.

There are reasons people lose their enthusiasm for life.

There are reasons God's people lose their hope, their sense of purpose, and their joy.

There are reasons life becomes just one long bore.

In my opinion, the foremost reasons are: (1) people have lost sight of who God made them to be and what He designed them to do; and (2) as a result, people are not actively, intentionally, and purposefully pursuing what the Father has planned for them.

If you truly want to pursue and reach your full potential, then you must face up to these two truths:

- Truth #1: God has placed more within you than you realize.
- Truth #2: You likely have settled for the life you have now.

ARE YOU LIVING A SETTLED-FOR LIFE?

Through the years, I have met countless people who are living what I call a "settled-for life." Someplace along the journey, they became complacent and content in their circumstances. They settled for what they believed was adequate or satisfactory.

A friend reminded me recently that several decades ago, children in the earliest grades of school were given one of three marks for their achievement: outstanding, satisfactory, or unsatisfactory. Children frequently compared their results, telling how many O's and S's they had received from their teacher. They never bragged, of course, about any U's. For most children, getting an S for satisfactory was just that—satisfactory.

S might also stand for settled for. If a student becomes content with a satisfactory effort, he will rarely apply himself to earn an O for outstanding.

The same is true in life. If a person becomes content with what is average, minimally acceptable, or satisfactory, she will rarely exert the effort or work toward something that is truly excellent or outstanding.

In the vast majority of cases, the longer a person remains satisfied with a string of S marks in her life, the more she becomes complacent about life. Going through the motions to achieve satisfactory results becomes the norm.

Eventually the person who has settled for a settled-for life may actually feel threatened by challenges to achieve, have, or experience more than what is presently the reality of her life. Ultimately she turns her back on her future and refuses to hope for more, seek more, or pursue more.

If that is where you are today, I encourage you to begin to see yourself the way God sees you. When you look at yourself through His eyes, you will no longer rest on the satisfactory marks of your settled-for life.

HOW GOD SEES YOU

You may be asking, "Well, how *does* God see me?"

Your heavenly Father sees you through eyes of love and forgiveness. He sees where you are, but more importantly, He sees the person He made you to be. God sees all the awesome potential and possibilities He created you to fulfill.

And if you are willing to discover and align yourself with His plan and purpose for you, He will bless you more than you could ever imagine. God promises to bless you with life at its best. He sees the restored joy, peace, and sense of accomplishment that He wants in your life.

Psalm 139 is a wonderful passage that speaks about the way the Father sees us.

> For You formed my inward parts;
> You covered me in my mother's womb.
> I will praise You, for I am fearfully and wonderfully made;
> Marvelous are Your works,
> And that my soul knows very well.
> My frame was not hidden from You,
> When I was made in secret,
> And skillfully wrought in the lowest parts of the earth.
> Your eyes saw my substance, being yet unformed.
> And in Your book they all were written,
> The days fashioned for me,
> When as yet there were none of them (vv. 13–16).

These verses from God's Word speak of three important truths about the way He sees you.

1. You Are Fearfully and Wonderfully Made

In God's eyes, you are fearfully and wonderfully made. Other translations of this verse from the earliest versions of the Bible use the words "awesomely wonderful." That's what the Father says about you. He has made you in a way that is awesome.

In the first chapter of Genesis, God says again and again that what He made is "good." Everything the Creator made was, at the outset, perfect in its form and in its function. It was beautiful, ordered, and magnificently connected to all other aspects of creation. It worked exactly as He intended it to work.

But after the fall, both form and function became warped. Each of us was born into a sinful world that isn't always beautiful and doesn't always work well or harmoniously. Nevertheless—and this is a vital point for you to understand—God said about your creation, "It is good." the Father made you for good purposes, and He made you with the potential to be *perfected* by His Spirit.

Does this mean that God will make you into the most beautiful woman or most handsome man on the earth? No. Rather, it means that He desires to engage in the process of transforming you from the inside out so that you are continually being molded into the most God-beloved, Christ-honoring, Spirit-yielded person you can ever be.

It also means that He is working all situations and circumstances for your good so that you can perform the functions He has equipped and enabled you to accomplish or complete during your lifetime.

God has an awesome, wonderful plan for you. The prophet Jeremiah explained it this way: "I know the thoughts that I think toward you, says the Lord, thoughts of peace and not of evil, to give you a future and a hope" (Jer. 29:11). The Lord has a great plan for you and created you to accomplish it in His name.

2. God Knows Everything About You

The psalmist wrote, "Your eyes saw my substance." Your substance is more than your flesh. It is the sum of all your natural gifts, talents, dreams, personality, and abilities. Even before you were conceived in your mother's womb, God saw you as a whole and unique person. He made you one of a kind, and from your beginning, He saw your ending. The Lord has always known what you could be and do, because He is the One who created you.

3. God Is the Author and Finisher of Your Days

The psalmist wrote that the days of his life were "fashioned" for him. You, too, were born at a particular time and to a particular family in a particular location. He made your life a set number of years in a set environment so you could be and do all that He created you to be and do.

Every person is born into circumstances with both good and bad aspects. Each of us will encounter a degree of evil and righteousness. We all will face the realities of death and life. God created you, equipped you, and then filled you with His Holy Spirit, to face every kind of situation. With His help and guidance, these situations will transform you from death to life, evil to good, and bad to best.

Your purpose on this earth is to develop your God-given gifts, talents, and abilities to the best of your ability so you can impact the world around you for Christ. In Matthew chapter six, Jesus taught His disciples to pray:

> *Our Father in heaven,*
> *Hallowed be Your name.*
> *Your kingdom come.*
> *Your will be done*
> *On earth as it is in heaven.* (vv. 9–10)

God has placed you in a time and location that will allow you to maximize your role in establishing His will "on earth as it is in heaven." You will do that through your prayers, your praise, your efforts to tell others about Jesus, and your work on His behalf.

If you have ever wondered why you are on this earth, understand that God has placed you here as a unique person with a unique mission aimed at establishing and extending His kingdom "on earth as it is in heaven." Your potential lies securely and completely in that purpose.

YOUR POTENTIAL LIES IN GOD'S PLANS AND PURPOSES FOR YOU

It is an awesome, eye-opening, and inspiring thing to catch a glimpse of how God is working in your life—weaving together who He made you to be with those things He has prepared you to do and experience. The threads of you as a unique individual are being intertwined with the threads of unique situations, circumstances, experiences, and relationships.

- He is bringing into your path people, opportunities, challenges, and resources.
- He is placing in you dreams, desires, and expectations about the challenges that already are winding their way to you.
- He is preparing you in every way for the many opportunities that lie ahead.
- He is setting within you the anticipation that something purpose-filled and exhilarating is just about to emerge.

When you begin to see the wonderful, prepared future that God is unfolding before you, life will take on greater importance and purpose. You'll wake up every morning with an excitement and a desire to experience all that He has planned for you!

On the other hand, you can miss those opportunities to see God at work in your life.

You can get so bogged down and so self-satisfied in your settled-for life that when the alarm goes off, you roll over and go back to sleep. You can become so complacent and apathetic that you become blind to the fact that God has more and more and more for you to be, experience, receive, and do.

- God has more ways for you to feel joy.
- God has more ways for you to experience His peace.
- God has more ways for you to encounter His beauty.
- God has more ideas to share with you.
- God has more expressions of love to shower upon you.

- God has an infinite supply of new mercies, new blessings, new accomplishments, new insights, and new inspirations to share with you.

As God's beloved child, you are in the hands of an all-powerful, all-knowing, all-loving, infinite Father who has divine plans and purposes for you—not only on this earth, but throughout eternity. There simply is no end to your potential when you serve an infinite God in an eternal heaven.

Our responsibility is to choose what He already has chosen for us. Repeatedly in His Word the Lord challenges us to "choose life." Again and again, God tells His children that He has set before us the possibilities of life. He wants us to embrace the life He has planned for us. This means that we must determine in our hearts and minds to live all our days to the utmost. We must welcome each new opportunity, grab hold of each new challenge, and face each new day with eagerness to discover what God has for us.

Furthermore, the Lord never holds before us an ordinary, mundane, merely okay, or satisfactory life. Jesus said, "I have come that they may have life, and that they may have it more abundantly" (John 10:10). An abundant life overflows with God's presence; it overflows with His love, joy, peace, hope, blessings, and power.

Are you passionate about life?

Do you deeply desire to experience all God has for you?

Do you really want His best in your finances, your job, your recreation, your hobbies, your relationships, your marriage, and your family?

Or have you settled for a settled-for life?

THE QUESTIONS YOU MUST ASK GOD

Have you ever stopped to seriously ask God about His will, plan, and purpose for your life? Are you fully willing and available to receive His answers? Among the questions I ask Him—and I encourage you to ask—are these:

- "What do You want to do in my life?"
- "What do You want to do through my life?"
- "What do You still desire for me to experience?"
- "What possibilities lie within me?"
- "What potential lies before me?"
- "What could I become?"
- "What did You have in mind when You created me?"
- "What do You desire for me?"

Only God can answer these questions. And for the vast majority of people in the vast majority of situations and circumstances, He will answer them only when asked.

Thousands of young people this very day are planning their futures—the job they want, where they want to travel, who they want to meet, the experiences they want to have. My questions to them are: "Have you asked God what He has created you to do and be? Have you asked the Lord what He has planned and purposed for you?"

But it is not only the young person who needs to ask these questions. Everyone needs to ask God these things periodically throughout life.

- The person who has recently lost a spouse
- The person who has been released from a job
- The person who has retired
- The person who is about to be married
- The person who will soon become a parent

We all need to ask God repeatedly and frequently, "What did You create me to do and be? What have You planned and purposed for me?"

FIVE KEY PRINCIPLES ABOUT YOUR POTENTIAL

The Word of God presents five key principles that are vital for our understanding of potential:

1. Every person has potential—no matter how much you may have achieved already and no matter how old you are. There's still more God has for you to be and do!
2. Every person has been created to bring God glory. How do we accomplish that? By being the people He made us to be individually and then collectively as His church. We also bring Him glory by fulfilling His purposes for us on earth.
3. No one can reach his potential without the Father's help or apart from our God-given talents and gifts.
4. No person can reach her potential without factoring in the spiritual dimension associated with it. God has not only created you with the gifts and talents to *do* His work on this earth, but He also has created you with the desires, dreams, and disposition to *become* a person with whom He enjoys fellowship and spiritual intimacy. Part of your potential lies in who God made you to be, not only in what He created you to do.
5. Only He knows the limits of your potential. You are finite and do not have the ability to fathom all that God has purposed for you. No one can fully understand the depths of His love, the help that He desires to give, or the blessings and rewards that He has prepared.

A person may reach the pinnacle of a profession or be lauded as the best in the world at a particular sport, skill, or craft. He may rank at the top of any number of the world's scales or criteria of evaluation. But unless he factors God into his life, seeking to love and serve Him whole-heartedly, he has not reached his full potential. He has maximized only his outward abilities and not his inward attributes.

YOUR POTENTIAL INCLUDES BOTH ATTRIBUTES AND ABILITIES

The difference between abilities and attributes is worth underscoring. Your *attributes* are your character traits—they are the real "you" that exists, regardless of external circumstances. They are the "you" that shows up no matter where you go or with whom you associate. The Bible gives us a very good description of the character that God desires to see in each of us. The apostle Paul wrote that it is the Father's purpose to conform us to the image of His Son Jesus, so that we might reflect Christ's nature and character to the world around us. (See Rom. 8:29.) That character is summarized in another of Paul's writings as being marked by "love, joy, peace, longsuffering, kindness, goodness, faithfulness, gentleness, [and] self-control" (Gal. 5:22–23).

These are not attributes that we can produce on our own. They develop in us as we say "no" to the flesh and "yes" to the Holy Spirit living and working in us. The Spirit matures us into the fullness of Christ's character. He generates in us the awareness, ability, and courage to live out a new life marked by godliness.

You cannot reach the full potential of your attributes apart from God.

The same is true for your *abilities.* You may think that by exercising, practicing, or pursuing education and training, you can reach the fullness of your God-given abilities. In truth, however, you cannot. The Lord gives you opportunities for developing your talents and gifts. He orchestrates your life to put you into the company of the right teachers, encouragers, and yes, even competitors—all of whom have a role in pushing you to achieve your full potential. But never forget that it is God who gives you the mental and physical energy to pursue the development of your talents and gifts. He is the One who provides your next heartbeat, your next breath, your next idea, and your next awareness of what is still possible. And God gives you the opportunities for displaying and using your talents and gifts in ways that produce true growth.

A wise university professor once told me, "Theory is great. The learning and understanding of concepts are essential. Rules, principles, and precepts are vital. But in the end, I know a student has truly mastered a particular subject or skill when that student is capable of performing well in a real-world setting. Learning is *completed* with application."

I couldn't agree more. The Christian life was never intended to be a matter of book learning or head knowledge. God wants us to live out the life He created and intends for us to live. The Bible tells us repeatedly to get knowledge and understanding. But then it challenges us to pursue wisdom, which is the application of knowledge and understanding in real-world situations according to God's commandments and principles.

But we must take a step beyond the mere application of what we know—that step is service. Our abilities are truly challenged when we manifest them in ways that genuinely help other people.

Let me give you an example. A young person may want to be a carpenter. He may have the physical aptitude to work with his hands, along with a certain degree of artistic ability that provides a sense of what makes quality, beautiful craftsmanship. He may work with a master carpenter to develop his talent and become highly skilled as a woodworker. As he develops his abilities, he gains an understanding of different types of wood, how to age wood, treat wood, stain or paint wood, or work with the grain of wood. Then the day comes when he completes a project on his own. As he finishes more and more, displaying finer and finer craftsmanship, his potential may appear to be realized. But from God's perspective, this carpenter has not reached his full potential until the day he turns his skills into service. Not until he builds adequate housing for a family living in cardboard boxes trimmed in tin, raises a church for purposes of worship, constructs a school for educating people in the truths of the Bible, or begins to teach others how to develop and use their woodworking skills for God's glory is his potential fully realized.

The same principle holds true for a young woman who has musical ability. She studies with excellent teachers, learns to read music, plays an instrument, or sings in a highly skilled way. The day for performance arrives in front of an audience in a way that wins their applause, perhaps even a standing ovation. But then the opportunity comes to use her beautiful voice or her skill as a musician for purposes that are truly evangelistic or worship-oriented. It is then that the fullness of her potential begins to be realized from the Father's perspective.

Only God provides those genuine opportunities for service, then rewards them with His presence.

Skills or abilities that are used in real-world situations for true service to the Lord give an added dimension to the word *purpose*. At this point, a person truly experiences fulfillment and joy.

Yes, God has placed within you the attitudes that will drive you to develop the right attributes that bring Him glory.

Yes, the Father has placed within you the aptitudes that can be trained and molded into the right abilities that bring Him glory.

And yes, God works throughout your entire life to bring you to the fullness of both your attributes and your abilities. You cannot do it in your own strength. You can do it only in God's strength and supply.

That is the reason I say with boldness: *Only God knows your potential, and only God can help you fulfill it.*

If you have never asked the Lord, "What do You want me to be?" ask Him that question today.

If you have never asked God, "What do You want me to do with my life?" ask Him right now.

EMBRACE ALL GOD'S POSSIBILITIES

The meaning of the word *potential* is very close to the meaning of the word *possibilities*.

Nobody knows fully the extent of the possibilities that God intends for your life. No one can look around the corner and see her life stretching all the way to heaven's gate. None of us can fully grasp his potential because no one can see all the possibilities that still lie ahead.

Neither can you know fully the ultimate potential or possibilities in another person's life.

You may watch someone play a particular sport or hear someone perform in a musical setting and decide, "That person has great potential." Something about the person's behavior or performance indicates that he has a certain aptitude to succeed in a particular area. The evaluation about potential is based upon evidence of talent or ability. The conclusion is that talent or ability is present, but undeveloped.

So what about areas that have gone unexplored in a person's life and, as a result, have no manifestation? What about the hidden areas of talent that have not been recognized or put to the test?

I am thoroughly convinced there are hidden talents, or what we might call latent natural abilities, in the lives of many people. These areas are present, but have never been realized. Or perhaps they were explored early in the person's life—perhaps in childhood or young teen years—and then they were suppressed. The talents may have been dormant for decades.

What about those abilities that have not yet been recognized, acknowledged, or in any way displayed, explored, or tested?

Only God knows the fullness of the gifts or talents that He has placed in you, and only God knows how He intended for those gifts and talents to be expressed in a particular time and place to fulfill His greater will, plan, and purpose. God knows exactly what He has designated for you to be and do in a precise number of years and in specific locations, working with and through certain people for the accomplishment of particular tasks and purposes.

Whether you are sixteen or ninety-six, the Lord has work for you to do!

THE POSSIBILITIES ARE ENDLESS

God not only has a plan in effect for your entire life—His plan goes on to future generations, all the way into eternity. Again, consider the life of the apostle Paul. What do you think went through his mind as he sat in a Roman jail? Do you think Paul knew that the letters he wrote from that place would continue to transform people's lives two thousand years later? God knew what the apostle Paul would never have imagined or anticipated.

There's no way to know how many people your life will influence. You don't know who is watching, listening, or learning from you. It's impossible to know for certain what those you influence will do, who they will influence, or how they will affect the world.

Every person impacts history in some way—for God or for the enemy, for good or for evil. What you do and say lives on in the hearts and minds of others, to some degree, with a definite result or consequence.

Are you willing to line up today with God's purpose and plan for your life and begin discovering what He still has for you to do?

Those who never discover and pursue His purpose for their lives very often feel disappointed, empty, and discouraged. They are frustrated, and, as a result, they frequently become anxious. If worry and anxiety are allowed to grow unchecked, they turn into depression. And if depression is not reversed, it can turn into deep despair. This downward spiral can be devastating.

The very opposite occurs in those who wholeheartedly pursue God's will, plan, and purpose. They feel energized, satisfied, and encouraged. They have hope and joy. They ride the waves of problems and challenges, believing that He is using those situations and circumstances to carry them forward to a greater good and greater trust in Him. The more they experience the Lord at work in them and through them, the more they trust God and grow in their intimacy with Him. This upward spiral continues all the way into heaven.

I once heard the story of a little girl who was walking on her toes throughout the house. When her father asked her, "Why are you walking that way?" she replied, "I'm seeing what it's like to be a big girl." God has a will, plan, and purpose for your life that should keep you walking on your tiptoes! He has even greater spiritual maturity for you, greater reward for you, greater joy for you, and greater success for you. And all of it, from the Lord's perspective, is so fantastic that you cannot begin to imagine how good it will be.

Do you really want God's best in your finances, your job, your relationships, your marriage, and your family?

Or have you settled for a settled-for existence?

Many people live at the level of good. As a result, they miss God's best.

Don't make that mistake today. Choose the fullness of the Lord's will, plan, and purpose for your life!

CHAPTER 3

READY . . . SET . . . PURSUE YOUR POTENTIAL!

Do you feel as if something is holding you back from pursuing your potential? Do you know what that "something" is?

Do you want to pursue your potential but just aren't sure that you can?

Or are you chomping at the bit to run the race that God has set before you?

Do you know what to do first?

It isn't enough to know that you cannot reach your full potential without the Lord's help and guidance. Specific shackles in your thinking may need to be faced and dealt with. God will help you correct your thinking, but you must make the first move.

CASTING OFF THE SHACKLES

Many people have allowed themselves to become shackled in their thinking in one of three ways:

1. They have made excuses for so long that they are bound up by them. The truth is that there are no good excuses for failing to pursue your God-given potential.

2. They have exempted themselves from pursuing their potential for any number of reasons. They have decided that their situations or circumstances are unchangeable and that nothing further should or can be done. In their minds, they have already reached the limits of what they can do. Or, they have arrived at the perfection of their character so no further refinement is needed.

3. They have condemned themselves for failing to ask God to reveal His plan and purpose for them. You may think you've missed it because you didn't seek the Lord's direction earlier in your life. Not so! You can discover and begin living according to His will, plan, and purpose right now. Start by asking God to forgive you for missing the mark in the past. Then pray for Him to show you what He desires for you to do now.

Let me remind you that Moses killed a man. Yet God used him to lead the children of Israel out of Egyptian bondage. And in his old age, he became one of the foremost figures of the Old Testament.

The apostle Paul—when he was still named Saul before his conversion on the road to Damascus—was not only guilty of murder; he had a self-appointed purpose of killing all Christians and destroying the church. But he became the most important missionary of all time.

Countless people in the Bible seemed unlikely candidates for the success that God led them to achieve.

Your past does not dictate what God is still able to do in you and through you in the future! Even if what you have accomplished in life is excellent by human standards, it is nothing compared to what God can do with your future. Never allow what happened yesterday to dictate what you will do tomorrow for God! Never rest on your past achievements and refuse to take on the challenges that lie ahead.

Cast off these shackles of faulty thinking. Embrace the awesome future God has for you!

SEVEN HURDLES TO OVERCOME

After you shake off the bonds that are keeping you from seeking and acknowledging your potential, you are likely to encounter several hurdles in your attitude or thinking. These obstacles can trip you up unless you are willing to overcome them with your faith. Let me point out at least seven of these hurdles.

Hurdle #1: A Limited Perspective

Some people are focused solely on themselves in the here and now. As a result, they are extremely nearsighted. They see only what is happening right before them or what is affecting their lives with the greatest intensity at any given moment. Concerned only with what is happening this hour or this day, these people live in the moment, sliding from minute to minute without any thought. They react to life rather than respond to it. Reactions are immediate, instinctual, impulsive, and generally arise from emotion. Responses, by comparison, are measured, evaluative, and "thought out" to some degree—and therefore, they tend to be slightly delayed in time. Both reactions and responses have a spiritual root but their expression is different. The Lord calls us to express godly responses—behaviors based upon our spiritual value system, our belief in God's Word, and our intimate relationship with Him.

Others view life by looking only in the mirror. They see only how people, circumstances, or situations affect them—not how they might impact the lives of others. Although these personality types do not consider others, they usually expect others to think continually about them and are upset if that is not the case!

If you believe that your purpose in life is solely in the here and now, or that your purpose is wrapped up entirely in what will benefit you, it is very likely that you will become extremely self-indulgent. You will ask only, "What brings me immediate pleasure and satisfaction?" And then you will seek out and pursue only those things.

The real question to ask is, "What does God have in mind for me and for my life?" Our ultimate purpose on this earth is not to gratify and satisfy ourselves, but to bring pleasure and joy to the heart of the Father.

Hurdle #2: Feelings of Low Self-Value

If you don't know that God has created you with promise—a hope and a future—you will not value yourself. If you don't know the promises and principles of His Word, you will not fully understand that He has been in charge of your life from before your conception. You will not know that every aspect of your being, every moment of your time on this earth, and every bit of influence that you might ever have on others around you has been authorized by God, has been planned by God, and is in the process of being implemented by God.

Not only that, but you are unlikely to value the lives of others. When I think of the millions of babies who have been put to death in their mothers' wombs, I shudder at the consequences for our nation and for those women. Why would a mother fail to value the potential and promise of her baby in her womb? Very likely because she fails to value the potential and promise of her own life. She may be ignorant of the fact that God fearfully and wonderfully made her with a plan and a purpose far more wonderful and important than she can dream or imagine.

God has given you a body with a degree of strength, energy, stature, and coordination. He has given you emotions and a capacity to experience and express them in a godly way. He has given you a need for love, an ability to receive love, and the capacity to express it to others. He has given you a mind and an ability to think, reason, and remember. He has given you an ability to communicate, both with and without words. He has given you a measure of faith, spiritual sensitivity, as well as a desire to know and be in relationship with Him.

God values you beyond anything you can fully imagine or understand. Consider all the galaxies and the stars and the planets moving through a universe so vast that we human beings cannot comprehend the edges of it. Think about all of the magnificent plants, animals, and formations on our planet, the seas and all that is in them, the patterns of sunrises and sunsets, and the beautiful palette God unfolds before us on a daily basis. Consider all that our Creator has made. None of it—let me repeat that—none of it stands in value to you. To God, one human being is worth more than all the rest of His creation combined. It is in you that He has placed the capacity to know Him, love Him, serve Him, and live with Him forever.

Even the angels stand in awe at what God has made available to you, placed in you, and provided for you.

As a human being, you have been endowed with the ability to express love to God and to receive His love. And only you can love God and receive His love in the unique way that He has planned for you before the foundation of the world.

No one else can relate to the Lord precisely the way you can relate to Him. In that, He is pleased and calls it good!

People have said to me, "Well, I don't see that I have the potential to do anything to serve God or to be used by Him to extend the gospel." A person who says that is looking at her life only through her own eyes, not

God's eyes. The Lord has made everyone with the potential to serve Him on this earth and to be a witness for Jesus Christ.

Hurdle #3: Constant Comparison to Others

One factor closely linked to low self-value or low self-worth is a tendency to compare one's success or abilities to those of another person. Very quickly, you might conclude, "I wasn't born into the family that person has," "I don't have the education that person has," or "I'm simply not gifted in the way that person is."

The truth is, you're right! You aren't like any other person who has ever lived, is alive, or will ever live. *You are one of a kind!*

The error in comparison is that we use our perceived shortcomings as an excuse for failing to trust God and pursue the potential He put in us. If we regard ourselves as failures before we even begin the race, we'll never run the race!

The apostle Paul wrote to the Corinthians that he did not fight against the difficulties of this life "as one who beats the air," which is a way of describing futility and inconsequential behavior. Paul fought the good fight to win it—to defeat Satan at every turn, to preach the gospel to the best of his ability, to go where the Father sent him, and to do what God asked of him so that he might win as many souls as possible. The apostle did not run the race of life with an expectation that he would never finish it. Nor did he run with a lackluster effort because he anticipated failing to win the prize. On the contrary, Paul wrote that he ran with purpose, certainty, and to win an imperishable crown. He disciplined his body and brought all aspects of his behavior into subjection to Christ so that he would be effective in reaching the goals set before him (1 Cor. 9:24–27).

Don't expect to fail.

Don't expect to be average.

Don't expect to fall short of God's goals for you.

Trust Him to help you win your race!

Always keep in mind that your race is *your* race and no one else's. God has set a course before you designed exclusively for you to travel; He has set tasks before you that you alone are to complete.

God has given you exactly what He intended for you to have as the basic tools, gifts, and abilities needed to fulfill His plan for you.

Hurdle #4: Self-Imposed Limitations

I cannot begin to know all the purposes and possibilities that God has for your life. But I do know that His ultimate purpose for you has nothing to do with your family tree, your school or college, your culture, your race, your financial and material acquisitions, or your personality. Your purpose in life is not something you achieve. It is not something man-made. Nor is it a situation into which you were born or grew up. It is not something that you have defined, are defining, or can define. God defined and planned your ultimate purpose. He set your ultimate purpose into place long before you were conceived in your mother's womb.

Your ultimate purpose is to bring Him glory by the way you live. God's plan is for you to experience great joy and fulfillment despite any hardship, trial, or difficulty that you encounter along life's path. He is calling you to persevere in pursuing His purpose for you and to grow in your faith and in your character every day and through every act of obedience.

Many self-imposed limitations are ones we carry from childhood. They are the results of what our parents told us we could or couldn't do. In some cases, they are rooted in cultural or religious teachings that told us life was nothing more than a series of rules and regulations to keep.

I grew up in a highly legalistic denomination. Life was perceived to be categorized into two very rigid lists labeled *should* and *should not*, with the emphasis placed on the should-not list. A person who grows up tightly bound by rules continually pressing in on every side has little opportunity to experience the freedom that comes with knowing Christ.

I'm not saying we are to live rule-free, commandment-free lives.

Rather, the rules and limitations that govern our lives are to be the commandments in the Word of God, not the theological or doctrinal preferences imposed by man.

Jesus faced this issue in His ministry. Most Jewish people in His day were considered unworthy of God's blessing because they did not keep all of the religious laws imposed upon their culture through the centuries. Literally hundreds of rules and regulations had to be kept if a person was to stay in right standing with God. Very few of these religious laws had anything to do directly with the Law of Moses in the Bible, and they were choking the faith of many Hebrew men and women. But Jesus said, "I have come to set the captives free!" (Isa. 61:1; Luke 4:18). He came to release them from their sin nature and from the legalism that had imprisoned their minds and weakened their faith in God.

Hurdle #5: The Fear of Disappointment

The Word of God says 365 times not to be afraid. Yet fear is one of the most damaging emotions believers face. A woman said to me about the fear of disappointment, "I just don't want to let down God or other people." I immediately responded, "Are you sure that your fear of disappointment isn't really a fear that God or other people will disappoint *you*? Are you perhaps afraid that if you open yourself up to the pursuit of your potential, God or other people may let you down in some way that keeps you from reaching more of your potential?" She admitted I was right.

So often we say that we don't want to disappoint others. But our greater fear is that we will disappoint ourselves or we will be disappointed by other people who fail to recognize our achievements, support us in our pursuit of God's purposes, or reject us for wanting more out of life. Some people fear that the Lord will be disappointed by their inability to fulfill His plan for their lives.

We need to face the fact that not everybody applauds the success of others. It seems that many people have a hard time truly appreciating or voicing approval. Jealousy and envy get in the way. Competitive behavior takes root. And before long, the very people to whom we looked for support seem to be the ones rejecting or criticizing us.

Let me assure you of these truths:

- God will never reject you, forsake you, or fail to encourage you as you seek to follow His leading and fulfill His plan for your life. He will help you, not hinder you.
- God is never disappointed by your sincere desire to do His will. He will uphold you, send others to assist you, and guide you to the path He desires for you to walk.
- God can turn all of your disappointments into joy. He has wonderful and unique ways of turning even the worst rejection into grand acceptance. He very often turns the harshest critics into the closest allies.

I have discovered repeatedly that people with a fear of disappointment are often perfectionists who expect too much too soon—both from themselves and from other people. The truth is, nobody can achieve perfection in this life. Each of us can do our best at everything we attempt, but no one is going to be perfect or do perfect work all the time. Furthermore, God has a timetable for the fulfillment of our potential. His will, plan, and purpose are revealed slowly and over time, day by day, step by step.

The older we get, most of us can look back at our lives and see how God's purposes have unfolded over time. If you and I have chosen to obey and live in right relationship with Him, we can look back and say, "I have done things I never would have thought I was capable of doing or would do. I have things that I never thought I would have. I have achieved things I never dreamed of achieving."

If we have chosen to allow the Holy Spirit to work in us to conform us to the image of Christ, we can also look back and say, "I'm not the person I once was."

Be encouraged by the work of God in your life! Adopting that perspective will keep you from being blocked by a fear of disappointment.

Hurdle #6: The Fear of Failure

Another major hurdle that can trip us up is the fear of failure. Each of us must acknowledge that we already have experienced far more failures than successes. How many times do you think you fell down learning to walk as a baby before you finally took your first steps? How many wrong notes did you play before you mastered your first piece on the piano? How many times have you misread driving instructions and taken a wrong turn?

All of us have failed at some things. But that does not mean *we* are failures. It tells us that we have tried some things and discovered that we needed more skills, more sensitivity, more love, more information, or more of God's presence and power in order to succeed. Failures teach us if we will choose to be taught. They inform us if we will open our minds to be informed. They guide us if we will open our hearts to God's Spirit for guidance.

In the world's eyes, Jesus was the biggest failure of all—a man who made exalted statements only to get Himself killed. Countless people around the world regard Christ as a good man who was martyred for His cause.

Jesus' closest friends abandoned Him on the night before His crucifixion. He was put to death in the most horrible and humiliating manner—hanging on a cross between two thieves.

The religious leaders of His day, the Roman guards at the cross, and the passing crowds saw Jesus as a failure.

But that is not the way God the Father saw His Son. And it is not the way we who believe in Him as Savior and follow Him as Lord see Christ. He is the One who died so that our sins can be forgiven and we can be in right relationship with God. Jesus is the One who rose from the dead so that we can live forever with our heavenly Father.

Failure is part of God's success formula! He does not exempt us from failing. Rather, He uses it to teach us and reveal to us what does not work as we pursue what will work. We know about the failures of Abraham Lincoln before he was ultimately elected president of the United States. We know the many failed attempts of Thomas Edison before he finally invented the light bulb. Failure is not only a part of life; God uses it to teach us what *not* to do. Every major invention, every major success has been preceded by multiple failures. In other words, you will fail at times as you pursue God's plan for your life. It is what you do with your failures that count. Do you deny them? Do you refuse to learn from them? Do you give up and refuse to try again? Do you allow them to discourage you to the point that you give up on yourself and on God? These are not the right responses to failure.

The best reply is, "Dear God, please show me how and why I failed. Help me not to repeat it, and enable me to get up, move forward, and trust You to work all things together for my eternal good."

Rather than focusing on the possibility of disappointment or failure, focus on the possibility of success. Focus on winning the race set before you. Focus on the rewards and benefits of a godly life of obedience and perseverance. Focus on the positive things He can accomplish through you and on the people who can be positively influenced by your example.

Those who refuse to take risks out of fear of disappointment and failure rarely experience the full joy and satisfaction that God desires for them.

Rather than focusing on what you can't do, haven't done, or have already failed at doing, focus on the fact that God has placed within you the capacity for success. He has prepared you for all types and degrees of achievement and accomplishment. God has built into you the ability to be complete and whole. He did not create you to partially succeed. He expects you to fulfill His purposes for your life, not to fail.

Hurdle #7: Laziness

Everything related to God's vision of success for your life is already in you. But if you are lazy, you will not make the necessary effort to explore or develop the gifts and talents that God has placed in you. If you are not willing to get up and get going on the tasks that lie ahead, you cannot experience the true joy and satisfaction that come with completing them to the best of your ability. Each of us faces a four-fold challenge about any task we undertake:

1. Productivity—doing as much as we can
2. Quality—doing things as well as we can
3. Time management—doing things as efficiently as we can
4. Maximum impact—doing things as effectively as we can

These four challenge areas automatically raise certain questions:

- Are you doing everything you can today to reach your full potential? Are you procrastinating, letting things slide, or avoiding certain responsibilities or tasks?
- Are you doing things in a slipshod manner instead of giving every task your best effort?
- Are you using your time well? Do you let your mind wander? Do you take unnecessary detours?
- Do you have goals that focus your efforts? Have you determined the area where God desires for you to have impact or influence? Are you continually looking for evidence that what you are doing is having significant results, such as making a positive difference in the life of another person?

There are no excuses for laziness.

GOD IS AT WORK!

Our heavenly Father is at work at all times, in all places, and in all people. Ask Him today to help you shake off all the things keeping you from pursuing your potential. Ask the Lord to help you overcome attitudes and beliefs that may appear as hurdles in the path of the eternal destiny He desires for you.

You cannot reach your full potential in your own strength and ability. You may have limited success for a limited time. But to truly leap over the hurdles I've described above and reach God's best for your life, you must have His help. And you must have it not just some of the time, but all of the time.

God will never deny you His presence or His purpose in the pursuit of your potential. Ask Him for help.

CHAPTER 4

ESSENTIAL #1:
A CLEAN HEART

D o you know with certainty today that you are in right relationship with God?

Do you believe you will have an eternal home in heaven with the Father?

Do you feel guilt or shame about anything? Or do you feel clean and forgiven?

Do you have full assurance that you have received Jesus Christ as your personal Savior? Are you following Him daily as your Lord?

This book presents seven essentials related to the pursuit of your God-given potential. But only one absolute essential relates to your eternal potential: you must have a clean heart. And by "heart," I am referring to your spirit—the place deep within you where you relate to God and experience His presence.

Why is a clean heart necessary?

You were born with a "bent" away from God. That is true for every person. All of us are born with a sinful nature—with a focus on self and self-gratification. Every baby clearly demonstrates this from its first breath—the cries of an infant related to human physical needs are insistent. Feed me! Change me! Hold me! Dress me! Comfort me! Do for me! It is a mark of maturity when a baby grows up to feed himself and care for himself. It is an even greater mark of maturity when a child begins to care for and give to others.

In the spiritual realm, we are also born with a focus on ourselves. We want what we want. We want the world to revolve around us. We want to determine our own destiny and to gain control over everything within our grasp. We want to know it all, be it all, and have it all. We seek only those things that will bring us immediate gratification. In our totally self-absorbed condition, a state called human pride, we have no desire for God. We do not want what He wants. In truth, we don't even want God in our lives unless it is to solve a problem or meet a need. More specifically, we call on Him to solve a situation that we perceive as a problem or to meet a desire that we call a need.

God sent His only begotten Son, Jesus Christ, into this world to die a substitutionary, vicarious, atoning death for us so that we might experience a change in our spiritual nature. The person who receives the sacrifice of Jesus as being on her behalf, and who believes in Him as Savior, has a new "bent." The Bible says that person is a new creature—a new spiritual creation—who is fully a part of the Father's immediate family (2 Cor. 5:17). That person is a son or daughter of the Most High God—a beloved child who will live forever in heaven. The person who accepts Jesus as Savior instantly receives the Holy Spirit to dwell within him and to enable him to *desire* a new way of living. The Holy Spirit empowers every new believer to *pursue* and live the Christian life.

Anyone living in human pride wants what he wants. He is living for himself. He may have goals and aspirations, but they are self-made and self-prioritized.

Some people who do not know Jesus as their Savior and Lord still set goals of helping other people. But note the difference—they set their own goals. They choose to help others because it makes them feel good. They establish their own definitions for a good deed and determine how much is enough when it comes to doing good.

The person whom God truly has forgiven and brought a change in spiritual nature enters an ongoing process in which his mind is renewed, redirected to walk the Lord's path, refocused in his desires, and reenergized to fulfill His purposes.

At that point, the Spirit begins to unlock and unleash the fullness of the person's potential. The Holy Spirit—the promise of the Father and the gift to every person who believes in Jesus Christ as the Son of God—unfolds before us all that we are created to be and to do.

Anytime you think, *I can't do this*, you must immediately reply, *But the Holy Spirit can and will.*

Anytime you think, *I don't know what to do*, you must immediately reply, *But the Holy Spirit knows, and He will lead and guide me.*

The Holy Spirit will not help us do anything that is apart from God's will, plan, and purpose. He will not empower us to do things that are of our own design simply because we think something is a good idea or a worthy project. The Holy Spirit helps us succeed at accomplishing all things that the Father calls us to be and do.

Until you have the new, cleansed heart that God offers you through forgiveness, you cannot fully understand the work of the Spirit. The unsaved person has no ongoing access to Him. But every believer with a clean and yielded heart is capable of hearing and heeding the voice of the Holy Spirit.

OUR CONTINUAL NEED FOR CONVICTION, CONFESSION, AND CLEANSING

The Bible admonishes us, "Do not quench the Spirit" (1 Thess. 5:19). To quench is to stifle. We are also told not to grieve the Holy Spirit (Eph. 4:30). To grieve is to cause sadness. What causes sadness in God? When we reject His love and His plan. Anytime we turn from the Father's way to our way, we grieve Him. Anytime we choose what we want over what God wants for us, we stifle the Holy Spirit's ability to help us.

Nothing grieves the Lord, and nothing stifles His work in us, more than disobedience. Sin—which is rejecting God's commandments—always causes us to miss the bull's-eye of the target He sets before us. Sin also results in us missing the mark and falling short of His best.

If we are to discover what God desires to do in us and through us, we must have the Holy Spirit's help. We must allow Him to enable us and empower us. We must ask the Spirit daily to cleanse us of all sin and to direct our attention, our minds, our affections, and our desires to God and His plan.

The truth is—you are only as clean as your last decision or choice.

Stop to think about that for a moment. You are only as clean as your last thought, your last attitude, your last unvoiced hope. Your need for the cleansing power of God's forgiveness is never-ending. You must ask the Holy Spirit to search your heart and reveal your sins so you can confess them and be forgiven continually.

We can learn from David's example as he wrote:

> *Search me, O God, and know my heart;*
> *Try me, and know my anxieties;*
> *And see if there is any wicked way in me,*
> *And lead me in the way everlasting.* (Ps. 139:23–24)

The psalmist asked God to reveal anything that he should confess before Him, anything that needed forgiveness. He asked God to show him how his life lined up with the Father's will, plan, and purpose—not just for the present, but for all eternity.

God knows what you should and should not do. He knows the best choice you should make and the best solutions for the problems you are facing. God knows what sin you need to confess so you can be forgiven and walk forward with a clean heart. Yes, your heavenly Father knows.

But do you know?

Do you want to know?

Do you really want to pursue God's best?

Are you willing to be changed?

Are you willing to yield your life to the guidance, counsel, and direction of the Holy Spirit?

Are you willing to live in a constant state of confession, forgiveness, and purity?

God's plan is His best for you. The Holy Spirit's job is to align you with that plan. His work is always for your eternal benefit.

THE BLESSINGS OF A CLEAN HEART

Jesus said, "Blessed are the pure in heart, for they shall see God" (Matt. 5:8). But He was referring not only to our seeing the Father in His heavenly throne room one day. Jesus was referring to our ability to see God at work in our lives right now—in our families, in relationships with people at work, in our friendships, and in our recreation and hobbies.

People who are pure in heart shall see God, not necessarily in visions or in the great spiritual exploits of others. But as He works in and through their own lives, they will begin to understand that the Lord is behind every good thing in their lives (James 1:17). The pure in heart will begin to grow in their understanding that God is working all things to their ultimate good—changing circumstances, bringing about unexpected events that produce unimagined benefit, and orchestrating relationships so that God's Word goes forth with greater power and more impact (Rom. 8:28).

Do you want to see more of the Father's work in your life?

Then pursue, desire, and seek a clean, pure heart.

Purity Is Possible—and Desirable

We live in a time when *purity* has become "old-fashioned." The world places a high value on tolerance, acceptance, and keeping an "open mind." But God's Word tells us to "be holy" and "keep yourself pure" (Lev. 11:45; 1 Tim. 5:22).

The truth presented in the New Testament is that purity is not only desirable; it is possible. The consequences of your sins are not just rolled back temporarily. Your very sin nature can be changed. On a daily and very personal basis, you can be cleansed from the stain of all your past, present, and future sins.

How many times a day do you wash your hands? If you are a physician, you likely wash them several times a day. If you are a construction worker, you may wash your hands only before a meal. No matter how many times you wash your hands, won't you still need to wash them again sometime in the future? Absolutely.

Do you wash your hands only when they are visibly dirty? No. You likely wash them before handling food or picking up a baby, even if your hands appear to be clean. You have studied enough in science class to know that some of the most harmful things to our health are invisible bacteria and viruses.

Most people take a bath or shower every day to stay clean. Nobody would want to be near you if you washed your hands and face once a week, brushed your teeth every couple of weeks, or bathed once a month.

If that were your hygiene routine, you'd probably find yourself fighting sickness and disease on a nonstop basis.

Yet people think they can go to church once a week, hear a few words of a sermon, read a verse or two of Scripture, and still have a clean heart because they acknowledged Jesus as their Savior at some point in their lives. In truth, the "soap" of God's Word hasn't even come close to "washing" their souls!

Maintaining a clean heart is a daily exercise.

Set Your Heart Toward Purity

The Bible tells us, "Keep your heart with all diligence, for out of it spring the issues of life" (Prov. 4:23). To "keep" your heart is to maintain its cleanliness with intention. To be diligent in something is to work hard at it, persevering in it with care and attention. The biblical understanding of the heart has very little to do with feelings and a great deal to do with intentions, motivations, desires, and will. The heart dictates attitudes and ideas. It gives rise to words and deeds that define your life. Your heart influences what you will to do, and then actually say and do. Your will is the foundational core for all your decisions and choices. Few things affect your present and future circumstances as greatly as your will. It dictates whether your life remains pure or becomes smudged by sin.

In very simple terms, having a clean heart and strong will are the prerequisites for living a godly life.

Sin, Confession, and Forgiveness Are Ongoing

God calls each of us to recognize our sin daily and to confess it quickly and openly. Then His Word tells us to request, receive, and accept the Lord's forgiveness (1 John 1:9). This same pattern applies to our trespasses against other people. We are to freely, fully, and immediately confess our sins when we recognize we have sinned, and seek forgiveness from God and any person we have offended.

To do that, of course, we need to know what God defines as sin. Indeed, the first step toward purity is to know what needs to be cleansed from us. A part of defining purity is defining impurity—knowing what is clean and unclean before God. To make a choice for purity, we must have an awareness that we are sinning and in what ways. Purity is not automatic. There are times, however, when sinning is very close to automatic—it is our basic instinct, our first response, our natural impulse, our fleshly desire in action. We must set our minds to do the right thing and choose what produces purity.

Some people believe they never sin.

They are in error.

We read in the Bible, "If we say that we have no sin, we deceive ourselves, and the truth is not in us" (1 John 1:8). Every person sins, even those who have accepted Jesus Christ as Savior and are born again. We all make mistakes and do things that we know we should not do.

Certainly the longer we follow Jesus as our Lord, the more we should mature spiritually. Christ redeems us from our desire to sin and the bondage associated with it. The Holy Spirit dwells within us to help us refrain from sinning and to convict us quickly when we do. Our first response must be, "O Lord, forgive me. Help me never to do that again!" But at no point in our earthly life are we beyond being tempted or unable to sin. As long as we live in human bodies, we are subject to physical desires that, if left unchecked, can lead us away from God's best.

Some people willfully do things they know are against the Father's commandments; others stumble into error totally oblivious that they are violating His law. Either way, they "fall short of the glory of God" (Rom. 3:23). Not only are there sins that people commit, but there are also sins of omission. This means not doing what should be done, or not knowing what should be done and therefore not doing it. While you may think you know the sins you commit, you will never know all the things you should have said or done. There will always be a vast number of your sins that are unknown to you.

For that reason, we must be quick to say often and sincerely, "Lord, forgive me for not knowing what I should know and for not doing what I should have done. Teach me; guide me; show me. Give me the courage to know Your will and then act on it."

We all have the opportunity to get "dirty" every day and to encounter things that can mar our souls and dull our spirits. We may not want to hear everything we hear. We may not want to see every image thrust before our eyes. We may not want to feel the anger, bitterness, resentment, or hatred that seems to rise up when a person does something that hurts or injures us or someone we care about. We may not want to make a bad choice or reach a decision that leads to negative consequences. We live in a fallen world and cannot avoid all of its temptations and traps.

While we may not be able to eliminate every outside influence, you and I can keep our thoughts from becoming impure fantasies or plans. We can say "no" the instant we realize that we are making a bad choice, are following a bad example, or are on the verge of giving in to a bad impulse.

We can refuse to harbor sin in our hearts. The Bible tells us that Jesus *redeemed* us by His sacrificial death on the cross. Through Him, we are no longer slaves to sinful impulses. In plain language, Satan no longer owns us or has a right to control us. We now belong to Christ, and He gives us, through the indwelling of His Spirit, the capacity to say no to sin and to harboring wrong impulses that may grow into full-blown desires and behavior. We have a capacity for resisting evil that unbelievers do not. We can say to the enemy of our souls, "I will not listen to you. I will not yield to you. I will resist you." The Bible tells us when we do this, the devil must flee from us (James 4:7).

Throughout the New Testament, we are told to resist the urge to sin. Do you think the authors of these sacred texts would have instructed us to do something that was impossible for us to do? The Holy Spirit enables us to turn from, put off, and resist evil whenever it comes against us. Believers can and must run to God whenever we are faced with temptation or recognize that we have sinned and say, "Cleanse me, Lord! Forgive me! Help me!"

Ask the Holy Spirit to help you—to reveal your sin so you can confess it. Ask Him to help you receive God's forgiveness, so you might forgive yourself and move forward in your life. Ask the Holy Spirit to defeat Satan on your behalf.

THE CONVICTING POWER
OF GOD'S WORD

In order to confess our sin with full understanding and true sorrow, we must first recognize that we have fallen short. How do we know what is a violation of God's commandments? How do we know that an attitude or an action is sin? The Bible presents such a clear statement of truth that when we line up our lives against it, our sin is obvious. God's Word reveals when we are not living the way He desires or commands. But the Lord did not give us Scripture so that we might run away in horror at our sin. Rather, the Word reveals our sinfulness so that we might confess our sin to the Father and be cleansed of it. The Bible promises, "If we confess our sins, He is faithful and just to forgive us our sins and to cleanse us from all unrighteousness" (1 John 1:9).

THE CLEANSING NATURE
OF GOD'S WORD

The Bible speaks of the "washing of water by the word" (Eph. 5:26). God's Word functions as a cleansing agent when you read it and seek to apply it to your life. It is the Father's "bar of soap" for your mind and heart. But it only works when you apply it. A bar of soap in your bathroom does not automatically make your body clean. You must take it out of the soap dish if you want to get clean. The same is true for God's Word.

Having a Bible on your bookshelf, occasionally carrying it to church, or opening it to read a verse now and then does not produce a clean heart in you. You must read the Word regularly and fervently.

Just as you wash your hands, face, and body daily, you must wash your mind and heart with the Word of God. You must spend time daily reading or listening to Scripture so that God's truth seeps into you and fills your thoughts. If you take in the Word daily, it will guard your heart and mind. Then, when you consciously or subconsciously come up against a situation that is tempting or wrong, you will be reminded, "Doing that, saying that, or participating in that does not fit my life in Christ. That is not what the Word of God presents as godly behavior that, in turn, brings the Lord's blessing. That is not something Jesus would have done or said, and therefore, it is not something I should be doing or saying."

The person whose mind is filled with the principles, precepts, and guidelines of God's Word has a level of understanding about right and wrong that the unbeliever can never have. Psalm 119 tells us:

> *Through Your precepts I get understanding;*
> *Therefore I hate every false way.*
> *Your word is a lamp to my feet*
> *And a light to my path.* (vv. 104–105)

A LIGHT TO YOUR PATH

My love of photography has allowed me to spend a significant amount of time hiking in some remote places around the world. When the sun sets in some of those locations, there is almost no light at all. If clouds cover the moon, or it is far from being full, the night can be very dark indeed. The noises of the forest or mountain areas take over your senses. The temperature drops. And if you have to leave your tent or step away from the fire, you must have a source of light to avoid falling down a ravine or worse.

A light along your path is essential for seeing three things:

1. *What lies ahead.* God's Word prepares you for future circumstances. It presents words of warning, wise counsel, and practical advice for dealing with challenges that are likely to come your way.

2. *What lies on either side.* The Bible gives you an understanding of the forces that are trying to pull you off God's path. It shows you the edge between what is acceptable and unacceptable to the Father.

3. *What lies immediately before you.* God's Word reveals the hole you are about to fall into, the snake you are about to step onto, or the rock you are about to stumble over. In other words, it enables you to see the things that can hurt you, destroy you, or slow you down.

THE POWER OF THE WORD APPLIED

As you read God's Word, you must continually ask yourself, *What does this mean to my life?* Ask the Holy Spirit to show you ways that Scripture relates directly to your situations, your immediate needs or problems, and your relationships. Ask Him to reveal what to do with the truth you have read—to show you how to live out God's Word in your world. You must listen for the Holy Spirit to bring various verses and passages to your mind as you face life's challenges. And always be on the alert for answers to these three questions:

- What does the Bible say about this?
- Who in God's Word has faced this situation, and how did the person respond and with what results?
- What does the Lord define as *godly behavior* or *right thinking* or a *good attitude* in this particular instance?

Allow God's Word to shape your attitudes, your emotions, and your thinking. It must become the way you feel, the way you respond, the way you form your perspective and opinions.

To pursue a clean heart requires intentionality. It means that you truly desire a clean heart and will do the necessary things to make a pure life your priority. Let me share with you some verses that are vital to maintaining a clean heart:

"I have rejoiced in the way of Your testimonies, as much as in all riches" (Ps. 119:14). God challenges you to voice praise for what you read in His Word. Thank Him for what He is teaching you. Let the Lord know that you value His instruction as much as His promises!

"I will meditate on Your precepts, and contemplate Your ways" (Ps. 119:15). God challenges you to spend serious, intentional time thinking about what He is saying in His Word. Casual reading isn't enough. You must absorb and understand all that the Bible has to tell you.

"Your word I have hidden in my heart, that I might not sin against You" (Ps. 119:11). God challenges you to memorize His Word and, at times, recall and recite Bible verses to yourself.

OUR MOTIVATION FOR PURITY

We should not be motivated to pursue a clean heart so that others will think well of us or so we can boast of being good people. All genuine motivation for obeying God must flow from our love for Him and our desire to be close to Him. When we truly love God, we will want to be as near to Him as possible—and closeness with the Father requires purity.

Psalm 119 says, "With my whole heart I have sought You; Oh, let me not wander from Your commandments!" (v. 10). The psalmist realized that to know God with the greatest depth of intimacy, he had to be obedient to the Lord. Jesus said that the first of all the commandments was this: "You shall love the LORD your God with all your heart, with all your soul, and with all your mind" (Matt. 22:37). Jesus also said to His disciples, "If you love Me, keep My commandments" (John 14:15).

The apostle John wrote, "For this is the love of God, that we keep His commandments" (1 John 5:3).

The best way to show love for our heavenly Father is to obey Him. Those who love God do what He says.

AN ONGOING SURRENDER
TO GOD'S WILL

God calls us to actively and intentionally yield our entire selves to His will on a day-to-day basis.

Among the last words that Jesus spoke to His followers before His crucifixion were these: "When He, the Spirit of truth, has come, He will guide you into all truth" (John 16:13). Jesus promised that the Holy Spirit would give believers insight into the mind of Christ, so they would know how to respond to any situation they faced. If those who had lived in close fellowship with the Savior for nearly three years needed the Holy Spirit's help, how much more do we need it? We must ask Him to reveal truth and to prompt us to live our lives as Jesus would—walking in righteousness, relating to others, and making choices as Christ would. If you have never turned over all your potential to the Lord, make this your day to say to Him:

Here's my life. I give it all to You. I surrender everything I have, everything I am, and everything I ever hope to have or be. Put Your plan into effect in my life. Forgive me, cleanse me, and use me in whatever way You desire.

A Life of Potential Pursued

CORINNE

Corinne bought into a dream that many young women her age were taught was a possibility: "You can have it all." Bright, beautiful, and very personable, Corinne went to college with the expectation that she would marry the man of her dreams, have perfect children, and have a career in which she rose to the top.

Well, she married. But her husband did not turn out to be all that he had presented himself to be. He had told her that he was a food service executive. Instead, he was actually the assistant manager of the evening shift at a sandwich shop. While there's nothing wrong with having that job, he had been in that position for five years and didn't aspire to anything else. Corinne confided in a friend, "He told me that he wanted a life that costs far more than what he would ever earn as a sandwich maker. What I didn't realize is that he expected *me* to earn the money for the lifestyle he wanted." Corinne blamed herself for not checking out his claims or his goal setting more closely.

By the time Corinne realized that she had fallen for a lazy man, they were already married. She threw herself into her career and tried her best to respect and love her husband with a genuine attitude of appreciation. Over time, however, she simply could not muster the good feelings toward her husband that she knew she should have. Corinne resented his constant insistence that she earn more money while, at the same time, spending her days watching videos and loafing with him on the dock of a nearby lake. Afraid she might get pregnant, Corinne decided to get a divorce.

But being divorced did not fit her perception of the kind of woman she had always wanted to be. She became depressed by the loss in her personal life, which ended up driving Corinne back to God.

She had accepted the Lord early in her teen years and had been faithful to the Lord throughout college. She had stopped going to church when she married and frankly didn't think she was worthy of Christ after her divorce.

But a wonderful Sunday school teacher spent dozens of hours with Corinne in the months after her return to church. She helped Corinne see that the most important thing in life was to have a clean heart before God. All other future pursuits didn't really matter if she didn't have a clean heart. Without it, God's true purpose for her life would not be fulfilled.

Corinne and her Sunday school teacher got down on their knees together one day after church, and Corinne asked God to forgive her—forgive her for the mistakes she had made related to her marriage, forgive her for having misplaced priorities, and most of all, for shutting Him out of her life. Corinne realized that she had been trying to succeed in her own strength and ability to gain all that the world said she should pursue.

Life changed dramatically in the aftermath of that prayer time.

Corinne felt more relaxed about her life than she had felt in years. She told her Sunday school teacher, "I no longer feel driven.

I realize I was striving for so many things, thinking that I had to accomplish certain goals within certain time frames, none of which were goals or schedules that God had led me to pursue. Now, I'm taking everything to Him in prayer every morning. I don't know what lies ahead, but I've given all of my life to God. I want all that He has for me and nothing that He doesn't have for me."

Is Corinne pursuing her God-given potential?

By all means, yes.

CHAPTER 5

ESSENTIAL #2:
A CLEAR MIND

Are you satisfied with just getting by in life?

Are you a passive person, accepting whatever is handed you?

Are you sitting by the highway of life watching the world go by?

Or do you want God's best in every area of your life?

Do you hunger to know what He might do in your life?

Do you have a passion for self-discovery—to test your limits and see what you might accomplish?

Do you desire to discover more of your talents and explore the full extent of your God-given potential?

Then, you must have a clear mind.

THE SPIRITUAL VS. NATURAL MIND

When writing to the Corinthians, the apostle Paul addressed the difference between the Christian and the non-Christian, between the spiritually minded person and the natural man. He wrote, "The natural man does not receive the things of the Spirit of God, for they are foolishness to him; nor can he know them, because they are spiritually discerned" (1 Cor. 2:14).

Many people who do not know Jesus think they understand spiritual matters. Millions around the world are on a quest seeking to be more "enlightened." But their understanding of spiritual matters is warped. They are actually in pursuit of false religions and false gods, including the god that they believe themselves to be. They are defining spirituality in strictly human, man-made terms. It is just as Paul wrote—they do not truly know the things of the Spirit of God.

The apostle went on to explain, "But he who is spiritual judges all things, yet he himself is rightly judged by no one. For who has known the mind of the LORD that he may instruct Him?' But we have the mind of Christ" (1 Cor. 2:15–16). What an awesome statement and an awesome concept! We who are filled with God's Spirit have the mind of Christ—not *will* have, but *do* have.

To have the mind of Christ means that we are able to perceive the world as He perceived it, to think the way He thinks, and to make decisions and choices He would make to bless us and bless others. I know very few people, even among my friends, who are spiritually mature and truly believe they have the mind of Christ.

When it comes to making a decision about relationships, they look to externals. They talk things over with their friends or counselors, weigh things against popular books of our age, and then decide. Rarely do I encounter people who go to the Lord about decisions in their relationships and ask, "God, is this the best You have for me?"

When it comes to making decisions about money, most people—including most Christians—look at the market trends and listen to popular financial gurus. They make decisions about their investments according to what man says, not what the Holy Spirit tells them. In fact, they rarely ask, "God, is this the investment You want me to make. Or is this the best use of my finances right now?"

The Bible tells us that we can know with certainty what the Lord thinks about an issue or opportunity. As believers, we have the capacity within us to think as Jesus thinks.

HAVING THE MIND OF CHRIST

The mind of Christ is spiritually discerning and rightly motivated. It is a gift of God to us. However, we cannot educate ourselves to have Christ's mind. In other words, we cannot go to some school and take a course or series of courses and emerge with some sort of certificate or degree that gives us the mind of Christ. We can only receive it if we are willing to accept what God desires to give us.

There are three major characteristics of the person who has the mind of Christ:

Characteristic #1: A Perspective of Wholeness

The person who has the mind of Christ perceives and thinks in terms of wholeness. Jesus did not heal specific ailments without regard to the rest of a person's life. Certainly He cured blindness, lameness, leprosy, and many other conditions, but He did so in a way that allowed a person to become truly whole. The Jewish concept of man at that time was much more integrated than our current concept.

Today, people routinely talk about the mind, emotions, body, and spirit as if they are four neatly divided and easily charted categories of an individual. We also tend to subdivide each of these areas so that we talk about bodily functions, attributes, and systems as if they are not connected to every other aspect of a person's physical being. We think that a physician is on the cutting edge of healthcare if she makes a connection between a person's thinking and his ailment.

Not long ago, a person introduced me to a ten-dollar scientific medical phrase that is easy to understand only if you break it down into much smaller parts: psychoneuroimmunological pathway. Basically, this means that what a person thinks (psych) impacts the functioning of the neurotransmitters in the brain (neuro), which in turn govern the production and function of the immune cells of the body (immuno), which regulate how the body responds to and overcomes invading bacteria, viruses, and fungi that can cause inflammation. If left unchecked, inflammation can set up in the walls of the circulatory system and be a major factor in heart disease, heart attacks, and strokes. In short, the way a person thinks has a very direct way—along an increasingly determined pathway—of impacting how and to what extent he or she becomes sick.

The truth is, God knew that all along. Jesus healed people in a way that not only removed the symptoms from their bodies, but it also set them on a path of thinking straight! He told the sick time and again that they had been "made whole" (Matt. 9:22; Luke 8:50; John 5:14 KJV). Jesus also told those He healed, "Sin no more" (John 5:14, 8:11)—which meant that He wanted them to change their attitudes, their thoughts, and their mental approach to life, in addition to their physical behavior.

The Bible is filled with truth on this subject. Proverbs 23:7 addresses this directly, telling us that as a man "thinks in his heart, so is he."

What does this mean to you and me as we make choices and decisions? It indicates that we must continually ask the Lord to show us the bigger picture. We need to ask, "How does this relate to the whole of my life? To the wholeness of my family? To the entire body of Christ?"

Our decisions become clearer when we consider them against God's plan for wholeness. What may seem pleasurable and right in the moment is suddenly and absolutely dead wrong when we become aware of the impact on other people or on our Christian testimony.

In addition to considering the impact of our attitudes, words, and actions on other people, we are wise to make decisions in the light of the whole of our lives. Too often we make choices that seem right for the current day, month, or year. We fail to consider how a decision might fit into the overall pattern of our lives or our spiritual growth over time.

After his wife died, a man in his late sixties suddenly began to make choices that were totally out of character for him. To look younger and be more attractive to women who were thirty-something, he began to dress differently. He rode dirt bikes on weekends and bought a speedboat for racing on a nearby lake.

Those of us who observed his behavior initially thought that he was acting out his grief or perhaps attempting to outrun his sense of mortality. One day a friend of this man said to him very bluntly, "Take a good look at yourself. You are not making decisions that honor Christ, and you are not bringing honor to your children."

The man was offended and reacted strongly to his friend's words. He defended his actions in terms of "my rights" and "freedom to do what I have always wanted to do" and "my happiness."

He included three very popular words in our culture today. I hear them all around me. People feel they have a *right* to do whatever they want without regard to others. They believe they have an inherent *freedom* to act in ways that are immoral, reckless, and at the very least inconsiderate. Still others talk about *happiness* as if it is the end-all and be-all of life.

Let me assure you, nowhere in God's Word does it say you have the right to do whatever you please. You are not given the freedom to hurt others, disrespect others, or violate the commandments of God. Scripture does not promise you or any other person uninterrupted happiness, and never does God call anyone to the pursuit of happiness. Be very clear in your understanding of happiness. It is a cheap and temporary substitute for the real joy that comes from having a solid relationship with God. Happiness is fleeting and based on outer circumstances. Joy is lasting and rooted deeply in the spirit.

Characteristic #2: Unity of Thought

Another way to determine whether we have the mind of Christ is to examine our thinking in terms of how concepts interrelate with one another. Too many people do not recognize how ideas are connected to other ideas.

Not long ago I encountered a person who told me three things in the space of a ten-minute conversation:

"I don't believe in abortion except in cases of rape and incest."

"Every baby conceived has a distinct genetic code."

"Stem cell research on aborted fetuses should be allowed legally."

I finally said to this person, "You can't have all three of those opinions simultaneously. They don't go together." The person looked at me as if I was the one being illogical. I pointed out that if a child is a unique human being from the moment of conception—with a one-of-a-kind genetic code—it really doesn't matter whether he or she was conceived in an act of violence or immorality. God authorized the creation of that child. The child is a distinctive human life and the mother can choose adoption after the baby is born, but her immediate responsibility is to provide a healthy environment for that unique human being inside her to grow to the point of a healthy birth.

Furthermore, stem cell research is proving to be much more successful using adult stem cells, especially stem cells from a person's own body, rather than the stem cells of an unknown placenta, umbilical cord, or fetal tissue. There is no scientific reason to pursue fetal stem cell research, which only reinforces our society's erroneous thinking about the acceptability of abortion.

Shortly after this conversation, I encountered another person who told me that she thought marriage needed to be totally redefined. Then in almost the same breath, she told me that she believed marriage was sacred before God. I said, "You can't have it both ways." Marriage is defined either by the Lord's standards or by man's standards.

When a person holds to opinions and makes statements of belief that are contradictory, her thinking is fragmented.

In contrast, the person who has the mind of Christ is able to develop a cohesive belief system. He or she is able to think logically and sequentially and to see how ideas or opinions are interrelated.

Characteristic #3: Creativity

The mind of Christ is creative in countless ways.

One great mark of creativity is the ability to put two good but seemingly unrelated things together to form something completely different but useful. This can be seen throughout our universe. For example, hydrogen and oxygen are both gases. But combine two atoms of hydrogen with one atom of oxygen and you get H_2O—water! Put that water in a very cold environment and you get ice. Put that water in a very hot environment and it becomes steam.

We are created by our Creator to be creative. God motivates us to see how things might fit together in new, beautiful, or useful ways. Just think about all the new technological gadgets, recipes, works of art, music, and more that continue to be created in our world today.

The mind of Christ is a creative mind.

A Combination of Traits and a Believer's Responsibility

When you combine these three concepts—wholeness, unity of thought, and creativity—you have the characteristics of the mind of Christ. As believers, we should work to bring about greater wholeness in our lives and in our world. Our thoughts should consistently and completely reflect a biblical worldview that points others to faith in Jesus. And our creativity must be used to display the glory and majesty of God.

IDEAS SHAPE YOUR LIFE

What you can conceive of as a child of God, you can accomplish as the Lord leads and the Holy Spirit enables. The Lord does not give us ideas to frustrate, confuse, or limit us. He imparts wisdom so that we might bring about changes in our world. God will use and enable us to carry out His redemptive plan to redeem lost souls and bless His people.

Into whatever service or ministry opportunity He may lead you, God will provide all that is necessary for you to succeed in the tasks He puts before you. His plan for your life will give you the greatest sense of joy and enthusiasm for what He has called you to be and do.

However, let me give you a cautionary word at this point. Many people have ideas and goals that are *not* part of God's plan. Most of them come down to a desire to be famous or wealthy. Those are not goals that He sets before us. They are illusions of the world that are held up to us as attractive and beneficial.

The person who seeks fame says, "If I'm famous, I'll be loved by people and have the love that's missing in my life." Those who seek fame often look at high-profile people and say, "They have it all." By "all," they perceive that celebrities, such as movie stars and professional athletes, have all the esteem, attention, applause, and love necessary for true contentment and satisfaction. In truth, many famous people feel extremely unlovable and would give anything to experience genuine, lasting love.

The person who seeks wealth says, "If I just have more money, I'll have power and influence." Those who seek money at any cost look at the world's "rich" and say, "They rule. They have power." In truth, some wealthy people may exert influence in a limited area, but if they are not spiritually minded, it can be more damaging than helpful. Consider those who have held great power over certain sectors of our financial markets recently. They made decisions that were far from the wisdom of God, and their wealth-based power was used in ways that brought great harm, discouragement, and loss.

The wealthy person may have value when it comes to a bank statement or a portfolio of investments, but this rarely translates into feelings of genuine worth. I know people who have pursued wealth in hopes that it would give them a feeling of acceptance before a critical father or mother, or that they would gain a sense of stability and security as their wealth and possessions increased. It hasn't happened, and it won't. True worth comes only when someone says, "God loves me and calls me valuable. He considers me worthy of His only begotten Son and trusts me to be His witness on this earth."

No, fame and wealth are not ideas that God plants in a person's mind. The more someone chases after those things, the more he or she needs to trust Him for guidance and wisdom. Fame and wealth will distract you from the fullness of your potential rather than enhance it.

The ideas the Lord plants in your mind are related directly to the talents He has already created in you and the opportunities He has already prepared for you.

Believers must recognize that God has given us the ability to do things that He desires to be done. We need to realize that God has promised to guide us along a particular path and enable us to do things far greater than anything we have previously asked or imagined. When that happens, God's people will find that we can hardly wait to get up in the morning and get going! Take my word for it—the enthusiasm that fills you will be contagious to others. You will experience joy at what you accomplish in a given day, even if no one sees you do it. But you'll know that your work is pleasing in His eyes.

THOUGHTS ARE AT THE CORE
OF YOUR CHARACTER DEVELOPMENT

How you think is directly related to what you produce and to the work you do. Your thinking also shapes your character.

Your mind is the control tower of your thoughts, attitudes, and beliefs. The combination of those three things determines what you will say and do. More specifically, they can dictate *how* you will express yourself. And what you say and do will impact your relationships with God and others.

Are your thoughts, attitudes, and beliefs directed toward having more or less of the Holy Spirit's guidance in your life? Do you want more or less of God's love? More or less of His joy and peace? His patience? Do you have thoughts, attitudes, and beliefs that create in you a desire to display greater kindness, goodness, faithfulness, gentleness, and self-control?

Your mind directs your heart with regard to what you desire to receive from God and who you desire to be before God. Your mind also dictates how your heart desires to relate to other people.

Do you have a mind filled with thoughts, attitudes, and beliefs related to winning or losing?

Are you focused on accomplishing something in life, or are you content to sit idly by while others do all the heavy lifting?

Do you have a mind filled with thoughts, attitudes, and beliefs related to gaining the fullness of God's blessings? Or are you just trying to hold on to the smaller portion that your limited strength and ability have enabled you to manipulate or control?

Look closely, and ask yourself, *What is the state of my mind?*

Your mind determines your level of success before God. It paves the way to your future. If you have wrong, natural, human-only thinking, your path to tomorrow will lead to disaster. If you have right thinking—which is godly, biblical, and wise—our heavenly Father will carry you to remarkable success.

WISDOM VS. INTELLIGENCE

Having the mind of Christ is not a matter of intelligence. I have heard people say, "I'm just not smart enough to think like Jesus thinks." They're right! No person is smart enough to think like the Son of God. We are all students who have learned how to think and what to think from teachers in school, in our families, communities, and churches. But none of those teachers was fully qualified to adequately instruct us in the absolute truth of God's Word.

Certainly the wisdom of the Father—which is the application of what to do in any given moment—is related to knowledge and understanding. The Bible calls us to grow in knowledge and understanding. We are to know facts and information about the world around us, including how it all relates to ourselves and other people. Believers need to have an understanding about the key principles that govern life. But in the end, wisdom truly makes the difference. Having wisdom is knowing what to do with what we know. It is the most important factor in applying what we read and study in God's Word. Wisdom tells us how to live out the truth that we receive and impart it to others for both their eternal benefit and earthly blessing.

Having the mind of Christ is not a matter of growing intellectually as much as it is a matter of receiving godly wisdom imparted to us by the Father Himself. To have the mind of Christ, we must ask the Lord, "Give me Your wisdom and insight into this matter. Show me what You want me to see. Tell me how You regard this particular situation or circumstance."

When we ask God for wisdom, He imparts it. The Bible tells us plainly:

> If any of you lacks wisdom, let him ask of God, who gives to all liberally and without reproach, and it will be given to him. But let him ask

in faith, with no doubting, for he who doubts is like a wave of the sea driven and tossed by the wind. For let not that man suppose that he will receive anything from the Lord; he is a double-minded man, unstable in all his ways (James 1:5–8).

Note these points in that passage from God's Word:

We are to ask. When we ask, our attention is focused on receiving an answer.

God gives us not only what we think we need to know, but all we need to know. He imparts wisdom to His children "liberally"—generously and completely—so that you and I are able to comprehend even those things we didn't know we needed to know. He reveals what is hidden and potentially harmful. He shows us what is beneficial yet just outside our ability to perceive it.

We must ask with faith. When we ask God for guidance, direction, or wisdom, we must ask expecting that He can, does, and will provide it. We must believe that the Lord will continue to guide us, direct us, and show us what to do as we walk the path He sets before us. And in obedience to God, we must be quick to act on what He tells us. You and I also need to be aware that the Lord has both perfect timing and a perfect method for everything He calls us or challenges us to do.

Part of being wise is getting confirmation about a course of action that you believe God is leading you to take. Look for that assurance in His Word, or seek wise counsel from others who believe the Bible and want the Lord's best in your life. Confirmation also can come as an idea or possibility that just won't go away. Clarity and conviction are related to asking for and receiving God's wisdom. The Father will not just tell you once what His best is for your life. He will tell you again and again, perhaps in a convicting or convincing way, and perhaps in an encouraging and supportive way.

Doubt makes us unstable. If we ask God for wisdom and then begin to second-guess what we believe He is telling us, we will be in an endless tug-of-war. We will repeatedly ask ourselves:

- *Did God really mean that?*
- *Did He say that, or did I make that up in my imagination?*
- *Did God really mean that, or is that just what I want?*
- *Did the Lord call me to do this, or did someone else plant that idea in me?*

People who say, "On the one hand," and then quickly add, "But on the other hand," rarely get anything done. For most people, doubt is not a lack of believing God as much as it is a failure to discern what He is saying. Some people truly believe that He does know best and can reveal His will. But they wonder whether they can know clearly what is God's will or His best.

The more you second-guess what you hear from the Lord, the more you will be paralyzed with doubt. You will be pulled in two or more directions, and as James says, you will be "double minded" and "unstable." What seems right today may seem wrong tomorrow.

You may ask, "But what if I make a mistake in acting on something that I believe is God's wisdom, only to discover that it wasn't?"

Again, the key to answering that question lies in receiving confirmation from the Father before moving forward. Check out what God speaks into your spirit against the whole of His Word. Does it line up with His principles and commandments? Is it consistent with the goodness and love of God? Will it influence others in a positive way to believe in Jesus as Savior? Does this action bless you, others around you, and ultimately the entire body of Christ?

God may not provide all the details and insight you need all at once.

But as you walk out His plan, and as you daily ask the Holy Spirit for guidance, God will take you from strength to strength, from one wise choice to the next, and from one inspired decision to the next.

Will you ever be omniscient—knowing all things? Of course not.

But you can have a very empowering relationship with the Holy Spirit, who is omniscient!

THE DOUBLE-MINDED PERSON

Double-minded people are forever changing their mind. They usually buy into and then repeat the statements of others in their presence whom they admire, fear, or are subservient to. A double-minded person says one thing in one setting and something entirely different in another. He changes his opinions or beliefs according to his circumstances or environment. In the end, the double-minded person doesn't really know what he believes.

God calls believers to make definite decisions about what, and in whom, we believe.

Stand on those decisions.

Choose the type of person you are going to be.

Make a firm commitment to listen only to God about matters of your identity. If something you hear about yourself doesn't reflect who you are in Christ, don't pay attention to it! If something you hear about God doesn't fit what you know about His true nature, don't buy into it!

Don't repeat lies you have been told.

Don't call yourself a failure when God says He made you for success.

Don't call yourself weak when you know that the Holy Spirit makes you strong.

Don't call yourself unworthy when God says you are worthy.

Don't call yourself stupid when you know that the Father created you with an incredible capacity to learn and receive wisdom.

If you call yourself what you aren't, you will be forever trying to walk on both sides of the street at the same time. You will be unstable and double-minded.

THE HALLMARKS OF A CLEAR MIND

A clear mind is able to see things as they are, not as they appear to be. It asks questions and seeks answers. A clear mind evaluates things accurately and does not draw conclusions too quickly.

We have all heard the expression: you can't judge a book by its cover. Most situations, circumstances, and people cannot be taken at face value. There's always more than meets the eye. There are things you don't see, don't know, and can't begin to comprehend.

Not long ago I heard about a situation in which a man suddenly and without provocation or reasoning told his wife that he wanted a divorce. She was shocked. His statement seemed to come out of the blue. Was there another woman? No. Was he upset about something his wife was doing? No. This woman's search for answers, brought her to the conclusion— along with her pastor, her husband's physician, and a pharmacist—that her husband had temporarily lost his good senses as the result of combining alcohol and a certain prescription medicine. The people who loved this man the most gathered around him to intervene and get him into a detox treatment facility.

At first, he hated what they had done. But as his body and brain began to heal in the aftermath of withdrawal from this highly toxic and highly addictive combination of chemicals, he recognized that his family and his professional associates had saved his life. He had come to the brink of poisoning his brain and his liver in ways that could have killed him in a matter of days if the situation had gone unaddressed and unchecked.

This woman had not known the degree to which her husband was drinking, nor was she aware of the excessive amount of prescription medicines he was taking. Confronted with his ultimatum about a divorce, she did not take his words at face value. She went on a mission to uncover the hidden truth and asked God to show her what was at the root of his behavior. This dear woman asked the Lord to show her how to respond to that root once she discovered it.

Don't assume to know everything about anything. You don't. But with a clear mind, you will know what you don't know and embark on a process of investigation and discovery.

A clear mind is not confused about right and wrong. A clear mind can differentiate between what is true and untrue, what is good and evil, and what is best and worst.

How do you reach this understanding? By reading and rereading the Word of God. Over time, right and wrong become clear. You can readily identify the truth. You can discern what is evil and what is good. You are aware that some things may be acceptable but not beneficial. And you know that God's best always makes the merely good pale by comparison.

A clear mind is not cluttered with vain philosophies, false religions, or worldly fantasies. The Bible tells us that even if we "understand all mysteries and all knowledge, . . . but have not love," we are nothing (1 Cor. 13:2). Yet many people are content to waste their breath on idle talk. Some feed on gossip, not only what they hear, but also what they read in print. They want the inside scoop—really, the inside scandal and sin—about another person's life. The truth is, that information is not at all helpful to anybody. Gossip brings no benefit to the person feeding on it, nor do those careless words bless their subject. Gossip hurts everyone.

Other people seek to know and discuss at great length things that have absolutely no eternal value. If there's no real meaning or godly purpose in something, set it aside and seek to fill your mind with what does have meaning and purpose. This includes some television programs you may be watching or books you may be reading. What is the lasting value of these pursuits? Are they worth watching or reading? TV shows and movies with visual images that are ungodly and detrimental to a person's character simply need to be turned off. They clutter the mind and are contrary to the Bible's command to meditate on things that are true, noble, just, pure, lovely, of good report, virtuous, and praiseworthy (Phil. 4:8).

A clear mind is unclogged by sinful thoughts. Some people think they should know about evil even before they are called to combat it. Therefore, they read about the occult, study false religions, or seek to"understand sin" by dabbling in practices the Bible clearly forbids. These misguided people think there is a degree of nobility and sophistication in knowing. But the more you seek out evil, the more likely you are to fall prey to it. Eventually the person who clouds his mind with evil images and ideas begins to fantasize about those things.

We do not need to know evil to fight it. Believers are called to "overcome evil with good" (Rom. 12:21). Our knowledge of God's Word is what really matters. And Scripture is clear that we are to "depart from evil" (Ps. 34:14, 37:27; Prov. 3:7) and "follow what is good" (Ps. 38:20). Sin corrupts everything it touches, including our thought life. It clogs our minds and keeps us from thinking clearly and correctly.

Ask the following questions about everything you choose to think about:

- Does this enhance my spiritual life?
- Does this promote my overall well-being and wholeness?
- Does this uplift, edify, or inspire me to greater good?
- Does this lead to holiness?
- Does this increase the work of God in my life?
- Does this add to my ability to discern good from evil, right from wrong, and to determine what is God's best?

If you hear or see something enough times, your thinking could be altered by it.

If you are told that something is acceptable enough times, you might be influenced by it.

That includes the messages that bombard your mind from various forms of media and from people who profess to know God yet do not have a true relationship with Jesus Christ. If you sit in a church pew and listen to false teaching long enough, you could be persuaded to think that Jesus was just a good man, not the Son of almighty God and the second person in the Trinity. The more you hear "liberal theology" question the supremacy and uniqueness of Christ, and see others around you nodding in agreement, the more likely you are to begin believing that what you are hearing is true.

Jesus said that false thinking and false understanding about Him would become rampant in the days before His return. He warned that even spiritually mature Christians would be in danger of falling victim to deception and error. Don't let it happen to you! Guard yourself against false teaching. Walk away from it. Don't listen to it. You don't need to know about it in order to refute it. Your best defense is knowing and speaking the truth.

Years ago, I learned how our government trains law enforcement officials to recognize counterfeit money. They spend countless hours studying real bills so they know the smallest details of true currency. These men and women never study counterfeit money. They know the real bills so well that fake ones are immediately obvious to them. The same is true for us. When we know the Word of God in its entirety and in its detail, we know false teaching the moment we hear or see it. The person steeped with God's truth will be able to immediately discern evil when it is present.

If you have any doubt about the truthfulness of a message you are exposed to, simply ask God, "Is this from You? Is this Your truth?" If a message is mostly true but partly false, He will label it false. Any bit of lie taints the truth. Don't buy into something because it seems to be mostly acceptable. That's the bait on the hook—something that seems a bit like the real thing. Don't swallow anything that isn't 100 percent true according to God's Word.

A clear mind is capable of maintaining focus. A clear mind stays on task and on track. Do you ever wonder why some people never seem to get anything done? It likely has to do with an inability to concentrate and stay focused on a job until they complete it. They are probably easily distracted.

A clear mind is capable of staying with a project until it is finished, studying for a test until the material is learned, or seeking an answer until it is found. Jesus said, "Ask, and it will be given to you; seek, and you will find; knock, and it will be opened to you" (Matt. 7:7). The English translation does not really convey the full meaning of these words. The better translation of the original Greek text would be, "Ask and keep on asking and asking and asking, and you will find the answer; seek and keep on seeking and seeking and seeking, and you will find; knock and keep on knocking and knocking and knocking, and the door will be opened to you."

If you cannot stay focused in your thinking, ask God to help you. Pray for Him to show you ways of removing distractions from your life. Try turning off some stimuli around you so you hear less noise and experience more of Him. Also, ask God to reveal to you the truth about the things you are allowing into your body—the foods you are eating, the beverages you are drinking, or the medications you may be taking. All of these can influence your ability to focus your thinking. It is always wise to talk to your physician about your medications or your eating habits.

Focus is inevitably tied to direction. Your focal point will determine where you will walk. Things that distract you will entice your participation.

If I announced, "I want to talk to you about something, but don't think about that big, blue, polka-dotted baboon sitting over in the corner of the room," you'd be able to think of nothing else but the big, blue, polka-dotted baboon.

A woman who says frequently and repeatedly, "I'm never going to date a man who . . . ," is likely to become so fixated on that trait that she will end up precisely with what she said she didn't want!

A man who frequently and repeatedly says, "I'm not going to be like my Father . . . ," is likely to become so fixated on the character traits of his father that he ends up just like Dad!

Direction is inevitably linked to God's will for your life. The Lord desires to direct you to the path He calls you to walk.

People have said to me, "I just can't figure out the will of God for me."

My answer is, "Ask Him to make it clear!"

After years of hearing people say they can't figure out the will of God, I have come to the conclusion that those folks aren't reading His Word as they should. If you read the Bible daily in a translation you understand with focused concentration, you are going to start understanding enough of it to make an impact in your life. The more you apply what you learn, the greater the difference the Word of God is going to make. Scripture makes the following very clear:

- the character we are to display day by day
- where our priorities are to be placed
- the subjects that are worthy of our study and learning
- which activities are good and which ones are bad from God's point of view

If we understand those things, God needs only to teach us directly about the details. Very often, He does that by leading us into opportunities that motivate us and match the talents He has given us. Therefore, they are opportunities at which we can and want to succeed.

If you don't know God's will, ask Him to help you concentrate on His

Word as you read it. Pray for Him to show you the character He desires to forge in you, the priorities He calls you to have, the kinds of thoughts He wants you to think, and the behaviors that He expects you to avoid. You'll be well on your way to knowing His will!

A clear mind is active, fruitful, and progressive. A clear mind is capable of learning and expanding. It can set godly goals and then form a plan for implementing them in the proper time frame.

A clear mind is capable of identifying good changes and pursuing them.

It has the ability to envision a better tomorrow and set out to make that happen.

A clear mind is capable of seeing the world the way God sees it and then working to make it function as He desires and intends.

HOW TO ACQUIRE A CLEAR MIND

The key to having a clear mind is to seek an intimate, personal relationship with Jesus Christ. We must desire to know and become like Him. He must be our Savior and our Role Model. We must receive what Jesus promised to give us—the indwelling presence and power of the Holy Spirit in our lives. He is available to give direction and guidance on a daily basis, and we must ask Him to help us, enable us, and empower us to live a victorious Christian life.

The apostle Paul declared:

Let this mind be in you which was also in Christ Jesus, who, being in the form of God, did not consider it robbery to be equal with God, but made Himself of no reputation, taking the form of a bondservant, and coming in the likeness of men. And being found in appearance as a man, He humbled Himself and became obedient to the point of death, even the death of the cross (Phil. 2:5–8).

Jesus had a very clear understanding of who He was and why He was on the earth. Our Savior regarded Himself as a servant. He humbled Himself before God and was obedient to all of the commands and leading of our heavenly Father.

That is God's profile for you. If you want to have the mind of Christ, you must see yourself as His servant on earth. The Bible calls us to be an ambassador and a bondservant for Christ (Eph 6:20; Gal, 1:2). You do what God leads you to do. He gives the directives, and you obey.

If you want to have the mind of Christ, you must humble yourself before the Lord and say daily, "Not my will, but Yours. I'm in submission to You. Show me where to go, what to say, and what to do."

Determine in Advance that You Will Obey

If you want to have the mind of Christ, you must determine within your heart to obey God's commandments. You will read the Bible and study it to the point that you truly know what He expects of you. Like Joshua, leader of the Israelites when they entered the Promised Land after the death of Moses, God's Word will bless and guide you. The Lord tells us in Joshua 1:8, "The Book of the Law shall not depart from your mouth, but you shall meditate in it day and night, that you may observe to do according to all that is written in it. For then you will make your way prosperous, and then you will have good success."

Let God's Word Program or Reprogram Your Mind

Brainwashing programs the mind through repetition. A message is presented again and again in association with something either tremendously positive or tremendously negative. The person undergoing the brainwashing will be pressured to embrace some desired belief or behavior that is inconsistent with his character or values.

Who is programming your mind? Are you going to the Holy Spirit-inspired Word of God to feed your mind with the truth? Or are you turning to another source to tell you what is acceptable and unacceptable—desirable and undesirable?

You cannot reach your God-given potential if you allow anything other than Him to define your world, you as a human being, or what is wise to take into your life.

A television commercial doesn't tell you just once that the product is good and worth buying. It repeats the information over and over. The product promises to make you more professional, more productive, more attractive to the opposite sex, more capable, more vibrant. My friend, no toothpaste, automobile, or beverage can do that. Commercials work by repetition and visual association with pleasurable things. People need to wake up and see reality for what it is!

Refuse to allow anything other than God's Word to define what is worthy, true, pleasurable, or meaningful.

Only the Bible can give you a right perspective and godly goals. Only Scripture can show you who you really are in God's eyes.

Reprogram False Teaching

The truth is, all of us were programmed or brainwashed as children to adopt certain thoughts and attitudes that we carried into adulthood. Some of what we were taught may need to be reprogrammed.

Who told you what you could and could not become?

Who told you how valuable you are and how lovable you are?

Who told you how much you could accomplish in life?

So many adults in our world today heard from their parents what they couldn't do, couldn't achieve, or couldn't be. They grew up hearing a father or mother say, "You're worthless," "I never wanted you," "You'll never amount to anything," or "Nobody will ever love you."

Those painful messages can be difficult to forget and overcome. If you grew up with negative, limiting parents, today is the day you need to say, "I was fed a pack of lies about myself." Start reading God's Word and come to a new understanding of how your Creator sees you. God says "You are loved. You are wanted. You are valuable. You have worth. And you have tremendous things to contribute to this world."

You don't need to rail against your past or your upbringing. Just start walking according to what your heavenly Father says about you and to you. Disregard the harsh, painful, and negative reinforcement of an ungodly parent.

As you read God's Word and take it into your heart and mind, the Lord will use truth to drive out error, lies, and falsehoods. He will minimize or erase all thought patterns that are unproductive and replace them with new ways of thinking that are beneficial.

Seek the Truth for Yourself

God will not infuse you with His Word by "divine injection." You must take charge of your understanding and open the Word of God daily. Read it and study it. Then believe it, and apply it to your life.

If you ever begin to question who you are and what you can do, search Scripture to see if what you are being told is true. If the negative things said to you don't line up with God's Word, say out loud, "I've been fed a pack of lies. I choose to believe the truth."

I know who I am. My name is Charles Stanley, and I am a pastor and teacher. There are things about me that you may know, but most of them you probably don't know. There are many facets to my life, and I have many areas of interest. But all of that is not nearly as important as the truth I know about who I am in Christ. Without any shadow of a doubt . . .

I know that I am a child of God.

I have been forgiven of my sins.

I have been redeemed from the bondage of sin.

I have been declared free of guilt.

I have been reconciled to God.

I am fully a part of God's family and an heir to all things that are for my eternal good.

I have been indwelt by the Holy Spirit, and He has sealed me to God the Father until the day I die.

My name has been written in the Lamb's Book of Life, and my ultimate home is in heaven.

Until that day comes, I walk as a testimony to the grace and goodness of God.

I am a member of the body of Christ.

I live to magnify Jesus Christ.

I relate to all other people and in all of my work in a way that seeks to bring glory to the Father.

I am a man on a mission to share the gospel of Jesus Christ with as many people as possible, as quickly as possible, as clearly as possible, as irresistibly as possible, through the power of the Holy Spirit to the glory of God.

That is who I am!

Do you know who you are in the Lord?

If you see yourself in any other light, go to God right now and say, "Father, set my mind straight about who I am in You!"

THE RENEWAL OF YOUR THINKING

The apostle Paul wrote to the Romans, "Do not be conformed to this world, but be transformed by the renewing of your mind, that you may prove what is that good and acceptable and perfect will of God" (Rom. 12:2).

The "world" as defined by Paul and other writers of the New Testament is a way of thinking and functioning. It is a system rooted in the pride of mankind and, therefore, is opposed to God at its core.

The renewal of your mind begins with an act of your will. You must actively determine and make a commitment in your spirit to subject everything you encounter in the world to the truth of God's Word. The renewal of your mind is found in submitting every thought or perception that captures your imagination to the Holy Spirit for His approval.

Your mind has the capacity to drift into all kinds of thoughts. Where you go and the people with whom you associate determine the types of messages your senses are going to perceive and translate into your mind as thoughts. You can be walking in the mall and suddenly see, hear, or smell something that triggers all kinds of wants, desires, and longings. Because you have already agreed to let the Holy Spirit be the final determiner about what sticks in your mind and what does not, you can rely on Him to convict you when a thought is not worthy of taking up permanent residence in you.

If the Holy Spirit says, "No, that thought doesn't fit who you are in Christ," you must immediately reject it. You may not be able to stop yourself from seeing a particular image, but you can refuse to "re-see" that image in your mind's eye. You may not be able to keep from hearing a particular song lyric, but you can refuse to sing it. You may not be able to isolate yourself from a particular temptation or experience, but you can make a firm decision not to entertain or develop a fantasy about it.

You can trust the Holy Spirit to prompt an impulse that says, "No, this is not for you." And if you are willing to say, "You're right. This is not for me and my life in Jesus Christ," you can count on the Holy Spirit to help you redirect your thoughts and attention to things that are for your good and that fit your true identity as a child of God.

At all times, the Holy Spirit will reinforce to you what the Word of God declares about the nature of a spiritual mind and the ways in which it stands in sharp contrast to a natural mind. Ask the Holy Spirit to engrave these concepts on your mind:

A spiritual mind is the opposite of a reprobate mind. A person with a reprobate mind has sinned against God so willfully and so often that he no longer regards his attitudes or behavior as sinful. What is bad, he says is good. He calls evil acceptable. What is wrong, he claims is right. There is absolutely no alignment between that person's behavior and God's description of good character. And the worst aspect of a reprobate mind is that the person with this thinking doesn't care that his life is totally opposite God's plan.

A person with a clear spiritual mind wants to pursue the Lord's will, plan, and purpose for his life because that is the best way to live.

A person with a reprobate mind becomes hardened in his thinking to the point that he defends his sinful behavior. It becomes not only justifiable and excusable, but also the correct way to live.

A spiritual mind is the opposite of a carnal mind or a fleshly mind. The carnal mind is focused on pleasure. It thinks about the lusts of the flesh, the lusts of the eyes (greed and materialism), and the pride of life (seeking power and control). It seeks out inappropriate and immoral images, literature, and messages to fuel carnal thinking.

A person develops a carnal or fleshly mind by focusing his thoughts on things that are subject to decay and degradation. Everything you encounter in life contributes either to your spiritual benefit and eternal reward or to your earthly demise and spiritual downfall.

You may not think that the images on your computer, in a magazine, or in a movie are defiling you. But the truth is, by looking at them, you are exploring, sampling, and participating in things that God says are unlawful, unhealthy, or unbeneficial.

Anytime your mind pursues objects or people in fantasies, daydreams, or wishful thinking that God cannot use for your growth and development, you are developing a carnal way of thinking. And that could lead to carnal actions. These sinful acts cause you to miss the mark that God has set for you and violate your relationship with Him. In the end, the pursuit of those behaviors will plant the seeds of death in you—the death of relationships, reputation, integrity, emotional and mental ability and capacity, and ultimately, the death of your body.

Avoid ungodly jokes and stories. Your mind can become cluttered very quickly if you listen to and repeat what is lewd, crude, or demeaning. Don't listen to or use racial slurs. Reject a spirit of criticism toward any group. Avoid judging people based on their gender, mental ability, physical disability, economic status, or any outward trait. Don't speak ill of people because of their personal attributes or physical characteristics.

A spiritual mind is the opposite of a hostile mind. A hostile mind is filled with thoughts that defy God and stand in direct opposition to Him. A hostile mind thinks, *I know I'm not thinking the way God thinks, but I'm right and He is wrong. I know how to think better than God thinks. My opinions and beliefs are right, and His opinions and absolutes, especially as stated in the Bible, are wrong.* Such a mind is actively at war with the Holy Spirit.

A hostile mind is angry and bitter toward God. A spiritual mind seeks the Father.

A spiritual mind is the opposite of a futile mind. A futile mind has determined that nothing will work. It says that nothing can be done, changed, redeemed, created, or accomplished. A spiritual mind believes for all things brighter, better, and godlier.

A spiritual mind is the opposite of a darkened mind. In John 8:12, Jesus not only calls himself the "Light of the World," He also says that those who follow Him "shall not walk in darkness, but have the light of life." A spiritual mind clearly sees Jesus for who He is and embraces everything that bears witness to the light of Christ.

The opposite is a darkened mind—one that the devil has so filled with lies and his oppressive, depressive, repressive spirit that the person is no longer capable of pursuing anything that gives testimony to Christ.

A darkened mind is the goal of Satan. He wants all people to come to the point that they have no awareness of God and no "light of life"—Jesus.

HOW YOU THINK
IS A CHOICE YOU MAKE

When dark thoughts or depression begin to creep into your thinking, you must choose to reject those thoughts and focus on the goodness of God. You can't dwell on His goodness and harbor negative thoughts at the same time. Choose the way you will think. Find and recite verses out loud from your Bible that speak of God's faithfulness and loving-kindness. Praise Him for His love flowing toward you.

When you begin to think that you are weak and will never be strong again, choose to think about the power and ability of God. He is in control of all things and reigns over heaven and earth with His awesome, omniscient, and omnipotent ability. Open God's Word and go to some of your favorite stories. As you read, consider just how "weak" or "lowly" most of the Bible heroes and heroines were *before* they were used by the Lord to accomplish great things. In truth, it is *only* as they trusted God that their lives took on great meaning or importance. Miriam was a slave girl in Egypt. David was a shepherd in the fields. Esther was just a young woman living an ordinary life. Nehemiah was a servant in the court of a foreign king. The list goes on and on. If you begin to think that you are all alone and always will be, choose to think about God's promise that He will never leave you nor forsake you (Heb. 13:5). Choose to think about the faithfulness of God. Read in your Bible about how Jesus promised not to leave His followers as orphans. Rather, He would send the Holy Spirit to bring them ongoing comfort and help (John 14:16–18). Praise God for being your Friend of friends, the One who is with you always.

If you begin to think that this world is hopelessly evil or that something negative in your life cannot be turned around, meditate on God's ability to conquer all evil and turn around every difficult situation and circumstance you face. Open your Bible and let the Lord's promises lead you along the path of a victorious Christian life. Read God's Word daily and praise Him as the Victor who frees you from ever being labeled a victim.

You Determine What You Think.

The National Science Foundation estimates that the average person has about 12,000 thoughts per day, which add up to approximately 4.4 million thoughts per year. You determine which thoughts will become actions. You decide whether to reject or accept an idea for further consideration.

Take charge of your thinking. Choose to dwell on things that fit your Christian identity and calling.

You Determine What You Will Recall for Contemplation.

You can choose whether to remind yourself of who you are in Jesus. Remember that God's Word says you have the mind of Christ.

You can decide whether to remind yourself of what Christ has done for you. The apostle Paul encouraged believer's to be strong in the Lord and to put on the full armor of God so they could stand against the devil (Eph. 6:10-11). He told the Ephesians to wear, among other things, the "helmet of salvation" (Eph. 6:17). A helmet protects the head. That was Paul's way of saying, "Put on what will protect and guard your thinking."

Think about what Christ has done for you. Consider what He purchased for you on the cross. Remember the forgiveness of sin and the freedom from guilt and shame that He provided for you by dying on the cross. Contemplate the eternal home you have in heaven because He has saved you from the eternal consequences of sin. Remind yourself that you are a redeemed, born-again creation of God!

Impure, demeaning, angry, bitter, resentful, lustful, manipulative, and greedy thoughts are not part of who you are in Christ. Don't relive your hurtful experiences. Avoid bringing them up from your memory to chew on them again.

Ungodly thinking doesn't fit the profile of a godly person, so turn off any ideas that could take root and lead you astray.

You Set Your Thoughts on the Way that Heaven Functions

The apostle Paul wrote that, as a Christian, you must "set your mind on things above, not on things on the earth" (Col. 3:2). Focus on the things that matter in eternity and that give life the greatest purpose and meaning in the here and now.

Think of Jesus. At the start of each day, ask the Lord to live His life in you and through you. Declare your intention to walk according to the rules and joy of heaven.

Even as you go through the routine of your daily schedule, you still can view life through the lens of heaven's holiness.

You can choose how to think much in the same way that you choose other things in life. You can decide to reject an idea and say, "That doesn't fit who I am!" You can turn your mind to another line of thinking and say, "Now this fits God's plan for me."

Choose to make the Father's perspective your perspective and to make His thoughts your thoughts.

A LIFE OF POTENTIAL PURSUED

DEREK

Derek loved cars. He especially enjoyed working with his dad and older brother on older automobiles. They would purchase these cars for relatively little money, then repair, restore, and resell them. It was a good side business for his dad, and Derek loved the challenge of seeing something returned to its original function and beauty.

People teased Derek all the way through high school that he was going to end up a grease monkey who worked as a mechanic at a car dealership or as an employee of a business that detailed cars. Derek rather liked both possibilities.

But a high school biology teacher opened Derek's eyes to another possibility. "You are really good at fixing things," the teacher said to his pupil one day. "I couldn't help but notice how you fixed that piece of lab equipment that needed repair. My guess is that you have really good mechanical aptitude and that you could succeed greatly as a mechanical engineer."

Up to that point, Derek had never even heard the term *mechanical engineer*. The biology teacher suggested that Derek see the school counselor to talk about courses he might find interesting and rewarding.

Derek had not even considered going to college prior to his conversation with his teacher. But now, he began to think about it. After several conversations with the school counselor, he made serious plans to attend college.

Eventually, Derek did become a mechanical engineer. While in college, he also took courses in biology, physiology, and anatomy. He became a leading designer of orthopedic devices to help people with degenerative bone and muscle diseases and had some of his inventions patented.

And he found that working with people who were struggling with their loss of mobility and physical function gave him tremendous opportunities to share his faith in Jesus Christ. Several times a week, it seemed, Derek had opportunities to pray with people who were either discouraged or in pain.

This mechanical engineer still enjoys tinkering with cars. And along with his teenage son Larry, Derek is again restoring automobiles. The father-and-son team regularly invites some of Larry's friends over to help them with engine repairs. Derek finds that these relaxed times of working with the young men on something very practical can provide opportunities for conversation—including discussions about Jesus.

"My message is always that it's one thing to be able to fix a car, but only God can fix the human heart," Derek says. "It's one thing to restore a car or even to restore mobility to a person with a serious injury or disease. But a person can only be fully restored to right relationship with God through Jesus Christ."

Is Derek pursuing his God-given potential?

Absolutely.

CHAPTER 6

ESSENTIAL #3:
USING YOUR GIFTS

Do you know what God has gifted you to do?

Are you functioning within your gifts?

Or are you trying to reach your potential through gifts you don't have?

Are you using your talents in the wrong way or in the wrong environment?

Do you enjoy practicing and using your talents?

An awareness of your God-given gifts, and the development of them, is a vital part of pursuing your potential.

If I handed you a hammer and then pointed toward a log and said, "Go split that wood and stoke the fireplace," you'd probably look at me as if I had lost my mind. Most likely, you would say, "I need an ax to do the job right."

If I gave you a screwdriver and asked you to saw a two-by-four in half, you'd probably say, "I can't do it."

Tools have been made and refined by craftsmen through the ages to be used for particular purposes. When a good tool is used properly, good work can be accomplished. When a good tool is used improperly, or the wrong tool is used, the results can be disastrous.

This same principle applies to the way in which God intended for you to reach your potential in life. He has gifted you in unique and wonderful ways. The Creator has crafted you with particular abilities and talents. When you develop those God-given attributes and use them to serve other people in love, great things can be accomplished. But if you try to function apart from your talents, or if you attempt to use your abilities in ways that God did not intend, you are headed for a life filled with anxiety, frustration, and failure.

Consider someone who wants to be a singer but has no musical ability. She may sing as loud as she can, but the result will not be a blessing to anyone who hears it. If she tried to sing, you likely would try to put as much distance as possible between you and her noise.

On the other hand, consider someone who is gifted in music and begins to develop that talent. Consider what would happen if that trained singer were to sing the kind of music that lifts your spirit. You would not only want to listen, but you would want her to sing again.

If you are going to reach your full potential in life, you must gain an awareness of what the Lord has given you. You must seek to know, develop, and then find God-approved ways to use your God-given talents.

Countless people today are doing things that God never asked them to do. They are striving to do what their parents want, what a teacher recommended, or what they thought they might like. They are attempting to succeed outside of their talent and ability to develop gifts that the Father has not given them.

There simply is no way you can succeed at something God has not gifted you to do. Furthermore, if you persist in trying to develop a talent you do not have, you will encounter a brick wall. God will not give you opportunities to go down a path He has not authorized you to walk.

Let me tell you about a fellow minister who has died and gone to heaven. In his early years, he felt a strong call to ministry and wanted to give his entire time, energy, and devotion to the church. He loved the people of God and wanted to see them succeed in reaching the lost and in raising up true disciples of Jesus who would go out and change the world.

This man was terrible at public speaking, however. Even though he went to a good Bible school to study the Word of God and took a course in communication, he could not seem to put together strong sermons— ones that either stirred people to give their lives to Christ or inspired them to make changes to better serve Jesus. Needless to say, he was frustrated by his lack of preaching and teaching success.

But he was even worse as a pastoral counselor. He didn't have the patience, nor did he have the compassion, for that work.

Still, he loved the church and wanted to serve God in it. Yet despite the sincerity and passion of his desires, he eventually was released from his appointment as a pastor. He was without a job and struggling to find his proper place.

In an effort to help this man support his family and regain his self-respect, a friend from the business world asked him to work for his company. He asked his new employee what skills he might have that could be used in business. The man replied, "I've always loved numbers and organizing things so they get done in a timely manner. I'm not very good at listening to problems that people may want to share, but I am pretty good at putting groups of people together to get specific projects done."

The businessman put him into an administrative assistant role, and within weeks, this man's financial and organizational skills came alive and began to bear fruit. Over the next few months, the former pastor led major reforms in several areas of the company. Things soon functioned more efficiently, with greater cost-effectiveness, and made better use of the company's resources and personnel. Task force teams he assembled became the driving creative force within the company. They made production lines more efficient and more profitable with higher quality.

This man worked in the business world for ten years. He rose to be the chief operating officer of a company that he helped grow to four times its size and increase its sales income by 600 percent.

Yet he still longed to serve the church. One day the pastor of a very large church approached the business owner and said, "Do you know anybody who could work alongside me as an administrative pastor—someone who can help us operate our church as successfully as your business operates in the manufacturing world?" The businessman was reluctant to give up one of his most valuable associates, but he knew it was the right thing to do.

The man who was a failure at preaching, teaching, and counseling became one of the finest administrative pastors in our nation. He worked in that area of ministry for more than thirty years before he retired. The churches that he helped grew substantially, functioned in great harmony, were financially sound, and launched dozens of ministries and outreach programs that reached hundreds of thousands of people around the world.

Knowing your God-given gifts and talents is vital to your potential. It is never enough just to enjoy something or to hope that you can develop a gift you do not have.

YOUR GIFTS FROM BIRTH

God has given you gifts and talents that He designed for you and bestowed upon you at birth. A true natural gift is present in a person all his life. I cannot begin to tell you all the natural gifts that are part of human beings. But I can encourage you in this: there are thousands upon thousands of natural gifts, many of which are variations within some of the general gift categories below:

Aptitudes

These are specific degrees of particular abilities related to your small muscle and large muscle coordination, the acuity of your hearing and eyesight, the sensitivity of your skin, your bone and muscle mass, your body's metabolism, and the reflexes of your nervous system. Every person has at least one aptitude. Most people have two or three. Few people have four, and very few people have more than that. Discover yours.

Intelligence

Intelligence is measured in many ways, but in general, you have been gifted with some degree of ability to process new information, to retain and recall it, to combine new data with old data, to apply it to real-world situations, and to generate new information. You have a degree of reasoning ability and of analytic ability. You have an ability to order your world spatially and conceptually.

Part of your intelligence is wrapped up in how well you think abstractly or theoretically—some people are much more concrete in their reasoning than others.

The truth is, most people use very little of their God-given brain power. You are capable of learning a great deal more than you probably think. Make the most of the intellectual ability you have been given.

Intuitive Ability

You have at least some ability to sense what is not visible and to imagine things you have never seen nor experienced. This "intuition" is not inherently godly or ungodly. But it does give every person an opportunity to experience God and create a void in everyone that only He can fill. The danger is that some people will think this ability by itself is spirituality. So they might begin to use it in ways that open them up to the occult. Stay within godly boundaries and allow your gift of intuitive ability to enhance your capacity to discern right from wrong.

Emotions

Emotions are gifts from God, which He intends for you to use in godly ways for godly results. You have been endowed with a degree of passion and a sense of justice. You have an emotional ability to respond to situations and circumstances with laughter and with tears. You have an emotional temperament that is part of your personality. Do not deny your emotions. But neither should you rely upon them to make sound judgments. Use your emotions to bring about positive change in your life and in the world.

Sexuality

You are either a man or a woman. And while it may be politically incorrect to say so, men and women are different. Scientific research confirms that the brain waves of newborn boys and newborn girls are not the same. Embrace your sexuality and know that it is a gift from God. That gift also includes a degree of sexual desire. Maintain your purity and holiness by living out that desire in obedience to His ways and commandments.

Talent in a Particular Area of Work or Performance

The Lord gives every person one or more talents. These are areas in which God intends for you to work in some form of service to others. Included among these talents are verbal and artistic creativity, craftsmanship, musical ability, teaching ability (which combines communication skills and learning), leadership ability, mathematical skills (abstract and concrete), strategic planning ability, and many more.

Interests

Every person has been gifted with a distinct set of interests. You may not have the ability to play an instrument or sing, but you may love music. Perhaps your interest will lead you to work with musicians or serve as a benefactor for a local symphony. Maybe you are interested in a particular sport or athletic activity. You may have an interest in travel, animals, or photography, as I do. Very often, your interests are related to areas in which God desires to use you. He could be calling you to explore or appreciate a particular aspect of His creation. Or the Lord may want you to become an encourager to those who have particular performance gifts.

In many cases, your interests will become the hobbies that give you an opportunity for recreation and relaxation. They could even become a vocation. Nearly always, your interests will draw you to a particular area of ministry.

Likes and Dislikes

Even young children have distinct likes and dislikes—in types of food, environments, music, in a desire to be held or not held, and so forth.

These gifts are unique to you in kind, number, combination, and degree. You may be a generalist—a well-rounded person with a number of talents, interests, and abilities. Or you may have just one area of talent that is intense and all consuming. I encourage you to recognize that not all people who are gifted in a particular area are gifted in the same way or to the same degree. Allow for variations within your friends and family members, while you acknowledge and allow for your gifts to be unique as well.

When you add up all the unique factors that are present in you from birth, there's no denying that you truly are a one-of-a-kind child of God. Nobody has exactly your set of gifts!

You also must recognize that you cannot change any part of your God-given gift set. You cannot feel what you cannot feel. You cannot think beyond your intelligence. You cannot trade one gift for another. God has made you with heights and depths that form a magnificent landscape. No one set of gifts is better or worse than another. All are made by God as part of His master plan for humanity. Embrace that wonderful aspect of your creation. You are *you*. Nobody can or ever will be you. And you should not desire to be anybody but you at your best.

EVEN MORE AREAS OF GIFTING . . .

In addition to the gifts noted above, God has given you and every other person the following:

Capacity. He has given you a capacity for learning, remembering, reasoning, and deciphering. He has given you an emotional capacity and a spiritual depth. Capacity varies from person to person.

Propensities. A propensity is a tendency to display a particular behavior. For example, some people are curious when faced with a new object or stimulus; others are fearful. Some people are quick to engage in conversation with other people; others are more shy or introverted.

Aspirations. God has placed aspirations within each person. This gift is a desire for something more and something great. Everyone has a dream.

Personality. Your personality has many facets to it, including your sense of humor, your attitude, your outlook on life, the way you respond to your environment, and how you relate to other people.

Free Will. God has given to every person free will within the parameters of His overall purpose for mankind.

A Measure of Faith. God blesses everyone with a measure of faith, which is an ability to believe in Him.

A Conscience. God has built within you the capacity to know right from wrong. He has a way of nudging your conscience, even if you haven't received godly instruction from your parents or anyone else during your early childhood.

Communication Ability. You are born with the ability to communicate. We learn and use languages that are both verbal and nonverbal.

A Network of Relationships. At birth, God places you within a group of people. It starts as only your family members but will grow to include the numerous friends, associates, and acquaintances you will meet over your lifetime. When you begin to see the people in your life as gifts from God, you will be much more willing to pray for them and be patient with them. He also gives you neighbors—people in your community and in your church.

Along with God's gift of people is His gift of culture to you. You were born into a setting with people who have particular customs, languages, traditions, stories, and histories. If you are a believer who grew up in a Christian home, your gift of people includes the entire lineage of biblical role models back to the time of Adam and Eve.

A Generation and a Location. You also were born into a certain time and space. The place where you were born—the location, the region, the geography of the land, the overall natural environment—was God's gift to you. That time and place also provided the advantage of various objects, situations, foods, styles, artifacts, music, and experiences that were, and perhaps still are, unique to that part of the world. You grew up in a specific house or dwelling in a preordained neighborhood and city. You were raised with specific sights, smells, and textures.

For those of you who moved around a lot as a child, I encourage you to see that God has given you a wide range of places and environments to call "home." It is a gift that has many benefits as well as challenges. The specific times you spent in each location are like pieces of a quilt that give your life texture and variety.

Nobody else on earth, not even members of your generation who grew up where you were born and raised, has precisely your context of time and space.

My friend, your uniqueness is absolutely mind-boggling. God has fearfully and wonderfully fashioned you from the first moments of your life. And once you catch even a glimpse of that, the more you will sense and appreciate the way in which God has fearfully and wonderfully fashioned every other person you encounter.

Contemplate what God has given you in each of these areas that I have mentioned. This may be some of the most valuable time you ever spend. Think about how you have been made. Focus on the specific talents and abilities that God has given you. Make lists for yourself about yourself. Do *not* write down what you think you should have or desire to have as gifts—write down those things that have been built into your life from birth. Do not list gifts that you think other people might want you to have. List what is. Construct a profile of your authentic, true self.

Ask God to reveal any hidden areas of talent or ability that you have not recognized in yourself. Sometimes the negativity of other people or the harshness of life's circumstances can smother or hide our giftedness from us. Ask the people who love you how they see your life.

After you've done all this, begin to explore ways that you can develop and use what God has given you.

STAY IN THE FLOW OF YOUR GIFTS

Once you discover your gifts, stay in the flow of them. I am well aware of what I am good at and what I have no business trying to become good at.

I can operate a computer to the point that it will do the things I need it to do. I can type words and organize them into a sermon or a manuscript of some kind. I can write letters and memos. But if you took the top off my computer, I would have absolutely no understanding of what I was seeing or how to fix anything that might be wrong. I am amazed by those who understand computers and their hardware.

I also am amazed that an inanimate set of wires strung together with bits of metal and plastic can make so much of the world's information accessible to us in a matter of seconds. What a fantastic age in which we live!

SEEK TO USE YOUR GIFTS IN CREATIVE WAYS

Only human beings are capable of asking key questions relating to creativity and invention:

"What might happen if . . . ?"

"What is the possibility for . . . ?"

"Could a person ever . . . ?"

The ability to create and invent is part of your God-given potential. Only you can string together the words you will say in your lifetime. Only you will have the insights that make certain aspects of your thinking and experience come alive with spiritual meaning.

When God authorized the building of the tabernacle for the Israelites, the Lord made it clear to Moses that He was calling particular people to be filled with "the Spirit of God, in wisdom and understanding, in knowledge and all manner of workmanship, to design artistic works, to work in gold and silver and bronze, in cutting jewels for setting, in carving wood, and to work in all manner of artistic workmanship." And those God was calling would be able to teach others to do "all manner of work of the engraver and the designer and the tapestry maker . . . and of the weaver—those who do every work and those who design artistic works" (Ex. 35:31–35). God has given only human beings the ability to be artistic solely for the purposes of creating beauty that enhances worship.

Yet man has distorted some of this artistic gifting and created things solely for the purpose of worshiping them. That was not the Father's intent. God gives artistic ability to people so they might create objects and works of art that enhance our worship of Him alone. The same is true for musical talent and all other talents we might say are part of artistry.

I strongly believe that every gift and talent has a creative dimension. Explore that possibility in your life.

GROWING IN YOUR GIFTS

In the natural, the best way for us to grow in our gifts and talents is through a blending of good teaching and a lot of practice.

Good Teaching and Training

You will develop your natural gifts at the fastest pace and in the best fashion if you are under the guidance of a good teacher or a strong mentor, trainer, or coach.

I encourage you to recognize the important difference between teaching and training. *Teaching* is the instruction of concepts, facts, principles, and general information. Most teaching is through verbal or visual means, and perhaps the best teaching is by example. A good role model is a great teacher.

The best teachers not only tell students what they should know and do, they also show their pupils a good example of what is being taught. Teaching is most effective when it leads to a genuine understanding that translates into practical application. Teaching ideally ends in wisdom. The student learns how and when to apply what he knows in ways that further God's purposes of winning souls and strengthening saints.

Training involves behavior. It is marked by repetition, practice, rehearsal, and drills. The Bible calls upon parents to "train" their children—to instill in them the repeated behaviors that will become godly habits that last a lifetime. Perhaps the most well-known verse about this is Proverbs 22:6, "Train up a child in the way he should go, and when he is old he will not depart from it."

You are wise to fill your life with good teachers and strong trainers.

Get the best information from the most knowledgeable source you can find. Seek out people who can become your mentors in specific areas of learning. Work with a trainer who can motivate you to practice at something until you acquire a skill. Refuse to stay with a teacher or trainer who is unwilling to tell you how to improve or how to correct error. The best teachers and trainers will inspire you to be your best and do your best. They can be tremendous assets in your life.

Some teaching and training is best done personally and privately. Other times it is appropriate in group settings. Still other teaching and training is possible through various forms of media. Once you reach your adult years, you have the responsibility to seek out the best teachers to help you develop your talents. Take advantage of every opportunity to learn from the most talented instructors you can find. When you were in school, others set the curriculum of required courses for you. Even after you finish all of your formal education, you can and must continue to learn. The good news is that you now have the privilege of establishing your own curriculum. You can study what you want to study. And the best subjects are those that fall within the realm of your natural gifts. That is where you will find your greatest satisfaction and success.

Much Practice

A very famous pianist in decades past always recognized his need to practice on a daily basis. He spent hours at the keyboard every day playing what many would consider to be rather boring scales. When asked about this, he noted, "If I don't practice one day, I know it the second day—and the world knows it the third day."

No matter what you desire to do, some element of practice is required for the end result to be excellent. No one is born with any ability that is fully developed.

Know your gift, get training and teaching related to it, and then practice it. You will quickly discover that most skills are developed slowly and incrementally. You may be discouraged some days, but stick with it and keep practicing. Very few skills improve with every practice session—some days you will see improvement, other days you may not.

True talent is worth developing to the point of mastery. When you have mastered something, you no longer have to struggle at it. You may work at it, but the sense of struggle is gone. There's an old saying that if something is worth doing, it is worth doing well. That's the goal in the development of your God-given talents. The Creator did not give you gifts to have you squander them, ignore them, or dabble at them. He intends for you to develop them to the highest levels possible

I strongly encourage you to make practicing your talent an act of praise to God. You may never have thought about it that way. But I have no doubt that you will gain much if you begin your practice times with prayer. Simply tell God,

"I exalt You, Lord, and I thank You for the gift You have given to me. I know You are the Giver of my talent, and I give You this session of practice as my gift to You today."

A young college-age musician was encouraged to think this way, and she later said, "I sat down to practice the clarinet, and I made a conscious decision to see that half hour as an offering of praise to God. I can only begin to tell you what happened. I played better in those thirty minutes than I ever had before. The more I saw myself as playing for God—like a private mini-concert just for Him—the more I found myself wanting to play with perfection and also with sensitivity. I thoroughly enjoyed my practice time and came away feeling absolutely great. I also felt inside me a greater excitement about playing the clarinet than I had ever felt before. It was an amazing time."

What about practicing your skill? Something wonderful will happen in you when you make it an act of praise to God.

While "*practice*" is another way of saying "*work*," the development of your gift will also be a source of immense joy for you. Few things bring greater satisfaction than knowing that you have tackled a difficult skill and mastered it.

Along the way, you fill find these concepts coming into play as you develop your gifts:

- *Diligence*. Practice must be regular and frequent. That takes diligence.
- *Discipline*. Practice doesn't happen by accident. You must plan for it and set apart time for it. You must motivate yourself to actually do it.
- *Perseverance*. There will be days when you will be discouraged by your lack of progress. You must persevere.
- *Consistency*. Practice is most effective when it is focused and scheduled as a regular part of your daily or weekly routine.

GIFTS THAT MOTIVATE YOU TO MINISTRY

In addition to the natural gifts that God gave you at your creation, you also received what I call motivational gifts to prepare you for and prompt you to ministry in the body of Christ. These gifts are released after you receive Jesus as your Savior and begin to follow Him as your Lord.

The apostle Paul wrote specifically about seven of these gifts in his letter to the church at Rome, "For as we have many members in one body, but all the members do not have the same function, so we, being many, are one body in Christ, and individually members of one another" (Rom. 12:4–5).

In his first letter to the church at Corinth, Paul wrote about how believers are all connected in the body of Christ, and yet each person has a unique role to fill and a unique gift for ministry. He explained, "There are diversities of gifts, but the same Spirit. There are differences of ministries, but the same Lord. And there are diversities of activities, but it is the same God who works all in all" (1 Cor. 12:4–6).

Note that Paul spoke of diversities and differences of:

- *Gifts*. These are the talents, abilities, and aspirations placed within us that "bend" toward a specific direction and function. These are given individually within the body of Christ.
- *Ministries*. These are the roles and functions that work together to edify and bless the body of Christ. There are specific things within a church that need to be in place for the body as a whole to be spiritually healthy.
- *Activities*. These are the specific tasks within a ministry. They are the ways and methods by which work gets done.

Paul wrote:

The manifestation of the Spirit is given to each one for the profit of all. . . . For as the body is one and has many members, but all the members of that one body, being many, are one body, so also is Christ. For by one Spirit we were all baptized into one body—whether Jews or Greeks, whether slaves or free—and have all been made to drink into one Spirit. For in fact the body is not one member but many.

If the foot should say, "Because I am not a hand, I am not of the body," is it therefore not of the body? And if the ear should say, "Because I am not an eye, I am not of the body," is it therefore not of the body? If the whole body were an eye, where would be the hearing? If the whole were hearing, where would be the smelling? But now God has set the members, each one of them, in the body just as He pleased. And if they were all one member, where would the body be? . . .

But God composed the body, having given greater honor to that part which lacks it, that there should be no schism in the body, but that the members should have the same care for one another. And if one member suffers, all the members suffer with it; or if one member is honored, all the members rejoice with it (1 Cor. 12:7, 12–19, 24–26).

Paul gave us a fantastic explanation of how the body of Christ is to function together, with each person contributing his or her gift for the benefit of the whole.

The gifts given by Jesus to His followers, which are released in us by the power of the Holy Spirit, have three characteristics that believers need to recognize:

1. Every person is expected to contribute. Each of us has been given a gift and a role to play. Everyone counts.

2. Our gifts are not for us alone. They are never given solely for our pleasure or enrichment. We receive them to us to prepare us and enable us to serve others. Every believer is expected to participate in ministry-related activities. There are no bystanders in the body of Christ.

3. Our gifts increase as we grow in Christ. Just as no one gift you had at birth was full-blown and ready for public display, no gift released within you when you were born again is fully developed. That does not mean you need to work for years and years to develop a ministry-related gift before you use it. These gifts grow and develop as you use them. They increase over time and through repeated application, but they only grow if you use them.

SEVEN SPECIFIC MINISTRY GIFTS

The apostle Paul identified seven motivational gifts that we are called to use in ministry or service within the body of Christ. He wrote:

> Having then gifts differing according to the grace that is given to us, let us use them: if prophecy, let us prophesy in proportion to our faith; or ministry, let us use it in our ministering; he who teaches, in teaching; he who exhorts, in exhortation; he who gives, with liberality; he who leads, with diligence; he who shows mercy, with cheerfulness (Rom. 12:6–8).

Let's take a moment to examine each of these gifts:

1. *Prophesying* is proclaiming God's Word. It is the foretelling of truth, and oftentimes it relates to future events.
2. *Ministering* is serving and helping to meet a need in another person's life.
3. *Teaching* is presenting information and principles from God's Word. It involves explaining how God desires His commandments to be lived out and applied to our lives daily.
4. *Exhorting* is admonishing and appealing to others to do what God has commanded. It is intense encouragement to live out the Christian life.
5. *Giving* involves practical expressions of time, treasure, and talent that are marked by generosity and faithfulness.
6. *Leading* may also be called administering or organizing. Maintaining a degree of diligence and consistency over time is associated with the ministry gift of leadership. But keep in mind that true leadership is ongoing and not limited to just one instance.

7. *Showing mercy* involves expressions of kindness that point to God's lovingkindness and His free offer of forgiveness, which is made possible through Jesus Christ.

Every believer has a gift within himself or herself "according to the grace that is given." God is the Giver of gifts, and through His Holy Spirit, He helps you identify, develop, and use yours. You do not choose your gift. God gives it to you. Your part is to recognize the gift you have been given, embrace it, and then seek to grow in it.

As you read through the list of seven gifts identified by Paul, you may have said about one of them, "That's mine!" Some people may have a secondary gift. But generally speaking, every person has a predominant gift that indicates God's intended purpose for him or her in serving the church.

Now these gifts are not formal ministry titles or job descriptions. In his letter to the Ephesians, Paul wrote:

He Himself gave some to be apostles, some prophets, some evangelists, and some pastors and teachers, for the equipping of the saints for the work of ministry, for the edifying of the body of Christ, till we all come to the unity of the faith and of the knowledge of the Son of God, to a perfect man, to the measure of the stature of the fullness of Christ. (4:11–13)

The roles he mentions—apostle, prophet, evangelist, pastor, teacher— are formal designations of leadership. These people equip others in the church to fulfill their work in ministry and to build up believers. God calls people to these positions, and in turn, He places them in particular bodies of believers. In turn, the church as a whole has a responsibility to receive and learn from them. If you were constructing an organizational chart for the church, you likely would find these roles at the top.

The motivational gifts noted in the passage from Romans function in clergy and in laypeople. These gifts do not flow vertically in a church. They flow laterally from one believer to the next.

DISCOVERING YOUR MINISTRY-RELATED GIFT

Some people have difficulty identifying their particular motivational gift. There are several reasons that Christians don't recognize them:

1. They may have a "cloudy" relationship with God. A man may not know that as a believer in Jesus Christ, he is indwelled by the Holy Spirit and has received a ministry gift. He may be unsure about his position in Jesus Christ. If any of these issues are relevant to your life, I encourage you to take action. Accept Jesus as your Savior. Recognize the Holy Spirit in you, and invite Him to teach and guide you daily. Study God's Word to discover your position in Christ.

2. They may not be involved in serving others. You learn much about yourself and your ministry gift as you reach out to help others.

3. They may be attempting to imitate another person. If you are trying to copy someone else's ministry gift, you are limiting the way the Holy Spirit desires to work in and through you.

4. They may be confused about the difference between a ministry and a gift. Ministry is a specific act of service to others. Working with the children's choir and feeding the homeless are two examples of ministry. A ministry gift is the motivation that leads a person to engage in a particular aspect of ministry. For example, someone who is involved in the children's choir ministry may have the gift of leading. Such a person is likely

to administer and organize the program and may very well be the choirmaster. Another person involved in the children's choir ministry may have a gift of service. They make sure that the choir robes are clean and pressed or that refreshments are available to the children after rehearsals.

In many cases, people have not considered how God has gifted their church's laypeople for ministry work. They tend to think that only clergy are ministers. But the Bible tells us that every Christian is a minister.

KNOW THE STRENGTHS AND WEAKNESSES

Every motivational ministry gift has both a dimension of great strength and a potential area of weakness. Prophets, for example, tend to be very bold and direct. The downside is that they can be so harsh that people refuse to heed their warnings or so judgmental that people cringe from their words.

God's Word makes clear statements about each gift and provides many examples of people who use them in positive and, at times, negative ways. The Bible gives words of encouragement as well as words of caution about the exercising of gifts. For example, the teacher must seek to be a good communicator and be open to new means of presenting information. But at the same time, he or she must avoid getting hung up on small details or a narrow perspective.

You need to study God's Word to learn as much as you can about the right and wrong ways to use your particular ministry gift. Discover what the Lord desires to accomplish through you when you apply your gift in service to others. As you study ministry gifts, you will find that each one is associated with a distinctive set of desirable traits. Below is an abbreviated list of those traits.

Gift	*Godly Expression and Traits*
Prophesying	Bold, persuasive, dependent upon Scriptures for truth, highly committed to the Lord, tender heart for people, quick discernment
Ministering/Serving	Alert, hospitable, generous, joyful, flexible, available, diligent in bringing projects to completion
Teaching	Ability to focus, reverent and respectful of God's Word, diligent and thorough, dependable, knowledgeable
Exhorting	Wise, discerning, faithful, discreet, loving, creative, enthusiastic
Giving	Thrifty, resourceful, contented, punctual, tolerant, cautious, thankful
Leading/Administering	Orderly, willing to take initiative and responsibility, humble, decisive, determined, loyal
Showing mercy	Attentive, sensitive, fair, compassionate, gentle, yielding for the sake of harmony and peace, willing to suffer if it will help another

JESUS IS OUR ROLE MODEL

Jesus is our Role Model for all ministry gifts. Only Christ embodied all seven in their fullness.

From one perspective, though, we are all to function in all the gifts at all times as followers of Jesus Christ.

Is there ever a time when we are not to speak the truth of God? No. We are to tell what we know of Him in every situation possible.

Is there ever a time when we are to refrain from reaching out to help a person in genuine need? No. We are to do all we can to help those whom God places in our path.

Is there ever a time when we should hesitate to teach someone who can benefit from knowing something we know? No. We are to freely share what we know about the Bible, the Lord, and the Christian life.

Is there ever a time when we are not to give? No. We may be led to support particular causes or people, and not others, but we are always to be givers. We are to give as much as we can in as many ways all the time.

Is there ever a time when we are to stop exhorting? Think of exhorting as encouragement rather than as telling someone what to do. We always need to be encouraging others to love and serve the Lord with all their hearts, minds, souls, and strength.

Is there ever a time when we should fail to lead? If you see leadership in terms of managing tasks, time, and people to get jobs done, the answer is a definite no. We are always to organize ourselves, our schedules, and our efforts in an effective and efficient way. You may not be called upon to lead other people, but you are always to lead yourself.

Is there ever a time in which we are to avoid extending mercy? No. We are always to be on the alert for people who need to know that God loves them, desires to forgive them, and has provided a way for them to live in a close, reconciled relationship with Him.

Each of us is gifted in one main area for service within the body of Christ. When attempting to use or apply that gift, we can and must look to Jesus as our Role Model.

Jesus as Prophet

Regardless of circumstances or consequences, He always spoke God's truth. Love was always His motivation, and the cleansing of human hearts and reconciliation with God the Father were His goals.

Jesus as Servant

One name given to Jesus was "Servant." Jesus taught His disciples:

> I have given you an example, that you should do as I have done to you.
> Most assuredly, I say to you, a servant is not greater than his master; nor
> is he who is sent greater than he who sent him. If you know these things,
> blessed are you if you do them. (John 13:15–17)

Jesus said this to His disciples after He had washed their feet—a lowly task usually carried out by household servants. As Jesus humbled Himself to serve, so must those who are gifted to serve. A true servant of God knows that no person should ever be considered too lowly or beneath them.

Jesus as Master Teacher

The disciples of Jesus frequently addressed him as "Teacher." He taught by example, illustration, and direct presentation of information. He was a consummate teacher in every way. Many of Jesus' miracles followed times of teaching. The Sermon on the Mount, which is the name given to the fifth, sixth, and seventh chapters of the gospel of Matthew, is a prime example of the way Jesus embodied and demonstrated good teaching. If you have been given the ministry gift of teaching, I encourage you to study all the ways Jesus taught, especially the parables of Matthew, Mark, Luke, and John. Nobody utilized that teaching device better than Christ.

Jesus as Exhorter

Jesus both encouraged and admonished those who followed Him. His words to the disciples at the Last Supper are a wonderful example of the gift of exhortation. He masterfully blended preaching and prayer. His message was interwoven with both promises and words of caution and rebuke (John 14–17).

Jesus as Giver

Nobody gave more than Jesus. He gave sacrificially, joyfully, and purposefully. He gave His life so that you and I could have eternal life. Jesus taught His disciples, "Greater love has no one than this, than to lay down one's life for his friends" (John 15:13). In obedience to the Father, Christ gave up His desires in favor of what God had authorized and directed Him to do. A person with the gift of giving must listen closely to what the Father is saying and fully obey Him.

Jesus as Leader

Jesus was not only the leader of a group of men called apostles and a broader group known as disciples. He is still the leader of His church. The apostle Paul said about Jesus: "He put all things under His feet, and gave Him to be head over all things to the church, which is His body, the fullness of Him who fills all in all" (Eph. 1:22–23). Jesus referred to Himself as the Good Shepherd of His flock (John 10:11, 14). He was a masterful leader in the way He organized His disciples, delegated authority to them, and empowered them to succeed.

Jesus as Bestower of Mercy

Jesus was the full embodiment of God's love. Christ was sent to this world as an expression of the Father's desire to be in a fully restored relationship with every person. God's Word tells us, "For God did not send His Son into the world to condemn the world, but that the world through Him might be saved" (John 3:17). Jesus did not merely talk about love or command others to love. He expressed love and gave love in the most generous and merciful way—He gave His life so that all who believe in Him can be forgiven of their sins and live in right relationship with God forever.

While ministry gifts are designed to be used together to build up the church, they function in all settings in your life as a believer. Whatever your gift may be, you can find ways to employ it in love, humility, and peace to those in your home, your extended family, your place of work, and any setting where you are in relationship with other people.

The godly use of ministry gifts is intended to bring glory to the Father. Make that your goal always. Exercise your ministry gift as you believe the Lord Jesus Christ would manifest your particular gift. Seek to do what He would do. Say what He would say. Always use your ministry gift in the fullness of the Holy Spirit: with "love, joy, peace, longsuffering, kindness, goodness, faithfulness, gentleness, [and] self-control" (Gal. 5:22–23). If you apply your gift in the true character of our Lord, you will bless others while reaping His rewards and blessings in return.

THE WAY WE EXPRESS ALL OF OUR GIFTS

All of our gifts—the motivational gifts for ministry and the natural gifts built into us from our creation—are to function in harmony with each other. Your gifts are to be expressed in the church with love, humility, and a peaceful attitude.

Love

We are to treat others with love at all times. Love must be our attitude, our tone of voice, the purpose for our actions, and the goal we seek in all of our relationships. Jesus said, "This is My commandment, that you love one another as I have loved you" (John 15:12). The apostle Paul provided this instruction: "Be kindly affectionate to one another with brotherly love, in honor giving preference to one another" (Rom. 12:10).

Humility

We are to treat others with respect, gentleness, and patience. Paul urged the Ephesians, "I, therefore, the prisoner of the Lord, beseech you to walk worthy of the calling with which you were called, with all lowliness and gentleness, with longsuffering, bearing with one another in love, endeavoring to keep the unity of the Spirit in the bond of peace" (4:1–3).

Peace.

We are to create an overall atmosphere of peace and reconciliation within the church. The ministry gifts are never intended to divide God's people. Rather, they are to heal, restore, nurture, unify, and build up the church into a strong and vibrant whole. The apostle Paul declared, "Let the peace of God rule in your hearts, to which also you were called in one body" (Col. 3:15).

Any exercise of our motivational gifts without love brings no benefit to us or others. If our ministry gifts are truly to be effective and be a blessing, we must choose to love, remain humble in our relationships, and work tirelessly for peace, understanding, and harmony.

When we use our motivational gifts in God-desired ways, we experience minimal frustration and maximum effectiveness. I certainly know that to be true in my life. Early in my work as a pastor, I was like many young men coming out of seminary. I was asked to lead a small church in a rural area of the country. I preached on Sunday mornings and Sunday nights and served as the Bible teacher on Wednesday nights. I also held every other job in the church, except part-time secretary. I made hospital visits, performed weddings and funerals, did pastoral counseling, organized all committees, and was the driving force for many of the various social activities. At times, I was both the transportation committee and the janitor. Let me assure you, there's no faster way to burn out. I am not surprised when I read statistics indicating that the majority of young preachers and small church pastors are exhausted and discouraged.

I also admit to having a feeling in those days that nobody else could or would do as good a job as I did. I was not very good at delegating responsibility or allowing others to use their gifts in service to the church. God had to teach me those lessons, and I'm so grateful that He did!

I am still very active in the administration of the church that I serve as senior pastor. But I know today that the most important thing I can do for my church and to honor the work that God has called me to do is to preach the best sermon I am capable of preaching on any given Sunday morning. That message eventually will go around the world and be broadcast in some form to nearly every nation on earth. It will be translated into dozens of languages and be available for study on the Internet.

Part of the reason I share that is to say this: my foremost motivational gift is exhortation. Some people call me a pastor with a gift of mercy. Others call me a Bible teacher. I relate to both roles very strongly. But from the core of my being, I know without doubt that my main ministry gifting is that of exhortation. My preaching challenges people to obey Christ, and I encourage them to obey God and leave all the consequences to Him. I trust that every message will convict those who need convicting, build up those who need to be strengthened, and encourage those who need to be encouraged to continue fighting the good fight of faith.

I know my gift and am never happier than when I am functioning in it. Preaching is not a burden to me. It is a joy. Preparing a message is not a chore to me. I delight in doing it because I am functioning in my gift. I sometimes spend as much as twenty hours preparing one sermon. That is the best possible use I can imagine for my time.

Does this mean that I don't get physically weary? No. I get very tired sometimes. Does this mean that I don't become discouraged when I haven't been able to convey my points as powerfully or as clearly as I had hoped? No. That happens on occasion—not often, but now and then. Does this mean that I don't need a break sometimes to rejuvenate and refocus my body, mind, and spirit? No. I do need breaks and am wise enough to take them. I need input and relaxation in order to have output that is effective and makes an impact.

The real danger is taking on too many responsibilities or commitments that detour me from my primary ministry gift. Life is filled with distractions. One of our greatest challenges is to stay focused and within the boundaries of the primary gift that God has given us.

I share all that to encourage you on the following two points:

First, as with your natural gifts, you must find and stay in the flow of your ministry-related gifts to be effective. If you get outside your gifts, you will end up frustrated and feel fragmented. The real strength of your ministry lies in your ability to say no to things that are not what God has gifted you to do. That's good exhortation for leaders in the church and for every person who calls himself or herself a Christian.

Second, you must not allow yourself to overextend your gift. If I accepted every invitation to speak, I could preach nearly every night of every year. That would last about three weeks, then I would be so exhausted that I would be worthless to fulfill the real opportunity that God has given me. Even if you are functioning fully within your gift, you need to take a break occasionally. In those times of rest, these things will happen: God will restore your energy and refresh your creativity, you will emerge more invigorated and stronger than before; and another person will have the opportunity to exercise his or her gift in your absence. That is part of God's plan for continually rejuvenating the body of Christ and raising up a new generation of leaders.

As we develop and use our ministry gifts, you and I find deep inner satisfaction and contentment. The purpose of our lives is fulfilled, and we have a great sense of meaning. To that, I can say a personal and hearty, "Amen!"

JOINING YOUR NATURAL AND MINISTRY GIFTS

In many ways, your natural and ministry gifts overlap. They enhance one another. Look and seek for that to happen.

God does not intend for any of the gifts He has given you to be used in anything other than a godly way—in godly service with a godly character and attitude. The gifts are to function as a whole in your life.

No person can teach you how to fully blend all of the gifts the Lord has placed and released in you by the power of His Holy Spirit. Only God Himself can teach you everything you need to know about your giftedness. Only the Holy Spirit can do the work of shaping and coordinating all areas of your life, so that they brightly reflect the light of the Lord.

Let me remind you that your potential lies in the arena of your God-given giftedness. Unless you are fully in the flow of what the Lord has created and authorized you to do, you cannot and will not succeed at accomplishing anything of value or eternal benefit. The very building blocks of your potential are the gifts He has given you.

I encourage you to memorize these words of the apostle Paul and recite them to yourself often: "We are His workmanship, created in Christ Jesus for good works, which God prepared beforehand that we should walk in them" (Eph. 2:10).

A LIFE OF POTENTIAL PURSUED

SAMMI

Samantha—known as Sammi to her friends—went to a minister friend of mine one day and said that several people had brought her this message: "You have a real heart for God, Sammi. I see how you praise and worship Him in the congregation. I believe God is raising you up to lead other people in praise and worship." Sammi asked if she could be part of the church's praise and worship team.

The pastor wisely told Sammi that there is an audition process for participation in the praise and worship ministry. Sammi agreed to sing for those in charge of auditioning. As you may have guessed, she choked in fear at the reality of singing by herself in front of three other people. Her fear was not normal stage fright or the kind of anxiety that can cause a person to perform at her peak. Her fear was knee-knocking, palm-sweating, inability-to-utter-a-sound fear. In the midst of the congregation, she could praise God with abandon because no one was watching her, at least no one about whom she was aware or concerned.

When Sammi finally was able to sing a few notes, her fear caused her vocal cords to constrict to the point that she sang horribly off key.

This story does not end in failure, however. One person on the auditioning panel stayed behind to talk with Sammi after the audition. They talked about what she enjoyed doing and about her relationship with Christ. They even discussed Sammi's talent to play the accordion. She laughed as she told the music minister how her grandfather had taught her to play it. Sammi said that although the accordion was considered a rather old-fashioned instrument and there were relatively few opportunities to play it, she loved the accordion. The music minister asked her, "Have you ever thought of playing it in praise to God?"

Sammi said, "No." The thought had never entered her mind. The music minister said, "Bring your accordion to church next Sunday, and after the service, play me a song."

Sammi did, and the music minister was astounded. When playing her accordion, Sammi had absolutely no stage fright. She played hymns and praise songs perfectly. In fact, she was the finest accordion player the music minister had ever heard. The church had never had an accordionist as part of its praise team before, but the team gathered together and made creative adjustments to several arrangements. Two weeks later, Sammi brought down the house with her rendition of "We're Marching to Zion," a classic gospel hymn that was familiar to many older members of the church.

Sammi was a gifted musician but not as a public singer. Nor was she gifted to lead a music ministry. When she was put into the right role for her particular gift, she succeeded. When Sammi attempted to do something she was not gifted to do, she not only failed but nearly missed the opportunity for later success.

CHAPTER 7

ESSENTIAL #4:
A HEALTHY BODY

Do you feel good in your body?

Do you feel healthy, strong, and full of energy?

Are your eating and exercise habits healthy?

You cannot reach your full potential, or even make a good effort toward pursuing it, when you are not right physically. Yet no factor seems to be more overlooked when it comes to your God-given potential.

A healthy body is critical to the preparation and execution of the various activities and ministry opportunities that the Lord gives you. You *need* a healthy body to fulfill your eternal destiny and achieve God's best for you.

We tend to think of ourselves as having body, soul, and spirit. Our bodies relate to other people and the world around us. Our souls relate to our personhood. And our spirits relate to God. When your body, soul, and spirit are strong and fully committed to the Lord, you can take dominion over certain aspects of the physical, emotional and spiritual realms.

Good health is absolutely necessary for the following:

- Mental focus
- Enthusiasm
- Clear thinking
- Motivation
- Perseverance to complete a task
- Quick response in times of danger, emergency, or crisis

Everything you experience affects your body in some way.

Someone may ask, "Well, what about those things that touch your emotions or that trigger a new thought in your mind?"

The truth is, your mind cannot function without your physical brain. You cannot think clearly if your brain is under the influence of drugs or alcohol or if it has poor circulation. In like manner, your brain does not produce all of the necessary neurotransmitters and hormones required for good physical health and function if your mind thinks depressed, angry, bitter, hateful, or otherwise negative thoughts. The mind and the brain are inseparable.

You cannot express emotion without activating your body. You express sorrow and suffering through tears. You are able to cry out in joy or pain through your lungs and vocal cords. Those who are very nervous or anxious display those emotions in their bodies. Signs vary from a nervous twitching or pinched facial expressions to larger, more obvious movements. Those who feel anger invariably and subconsciously tend to clench their fists and tighten their jaw muscles.

There is tremendous healing power in touch. People need appropriate ways of physical contact as a part of prayer and as a way of expressing encouragement and affection. Children need to be held and cuddled. Adults never lose their need to be hugged. From time to time, they also need a pat on the back or a hand extended in help.

Every experience, idea, and emotion that you encounter is internalized in some way in your body. Furthermore, how you affect your world and others around you is expressed through your physical body.

Gestures—whether facial or hand—communicate volumes. The way you sit, walk, and stand sends a message to people. The smile on your face, the twinkle in your eyes, the gentleness of your touch, the words from your lips—all communicate and have impact. The words that you speak are projected through various body parts in a way that sends sound waves to the ears of others. You go places in your physical body. You meet people in the flesh.

Why am I emphasizing these points? Because too often we tend to think that only what happens in the spirit matters in spreading the gospel and in the church. The greater truth is that what we do with our bodies greatly influences the Great Commission and the body of Christ.

On occasion people have said to me, "I can't come to church next Sunday, but I'll be with you in spirit." I try to hold back what I'm thinking, but sometimes I'm not very good at it. My first response is likely to be, "No, you're not." You can't send your spirit somewhere. You are not going to be with us in church in your spirit unless your spirit walks through the door of the church inside your body. My more polite response is, "I'd rather have your body here. It can smile and shake hands with folks around you. It is with your physical voice that you can join in singing and saying, 'Amen!' Your spirit apart from your body can't do any of that." And I can guarantee you that your spirit won't reach down into your pocket that's not there and put something into the offering plate. Neither will your spirit function in any gift that edifies other believers or witnesses to lost souls apart from your body.

GOD'S CLAIM TO YOUR BODY

Writing to the Corinthians, the apostle Paul discussed the body:

> All things are lawful for me, but all things are not helpful. All things are
> lawful for me, but I will not be brought under the power of any. Foods
> for the stomach and the stomach for foods, but God will destroy both it
> and them. Now the body is not for sexual immorality but for the Lord,
> and the Lord for the body. And God both raised up the Lord and will
> also raise us up by His power.

He added, "Do you not know that your body is the temple of the Holy
Spirit who is in you, whom you have from God, and you are not your
own? For you were bought at a price; therefore glorify God in your body
and in your spirit, which are God's" (1 Cor. 6:12–14, 19–20).

Paul wrote this passage against a backdrop of an ongoing discussion
he had with many churches in the Roman Empire where idolatry and
idol worship were rampant. The real issue behind his words was whether
Christians could eat foods that had first been sacrificed to idols.

The custom in the pagan temples was for people to bring offerings
of meat, wine, and produce to various idols there. After a brief period,
these items were removed from their position before the idol and put
into a market where the food could be purchased by anyone who wanted
to buy it. The belief underlying this custom was that the person making
the offering was joining with the idol in a feast. There was a concept of
identifying with the idol in this supposed sharing of food. Believers questioned whether it was right before God for them to purchase food from
the temple market.

Paul's argument was very plain to them—idols aren't real. They don't
eat the food offered to them, not in the natural or spirit realm. Therefore,
the meat is untainted by any demonic spirit and is acceptable for purchase.

But Paul also said that if the purchase of this food became a stumbling block to someone's faith, they should avoid it. Eating meat or not eating meat offered to idols was not the real issue. The real issue was whether or not a person was acting in a manner that built up another's faith or paved the way for an unbeliever to receive Jesus Christ as his personal Savior.

The Corinthians loved this idea of personal freedom, and some began to wonder if other practices in the pagan temples were allowable. Part of the false religion practiced by the Greeks and Romans provided for fertility-oriented rituals to be performed between temple-hired prostitutes and ordinary citizens. The pagan thinking was that a man could have sex with a temple prostitute as an act of worship to the god that governed harvests or fertility. Then the god would grant the man a good harvest of his crops, increased birth rates for his sheep, goats, and cattle, and more children from his wife or wives.

Paul was quick to put a stop to any speculation about whether these sexual acts were appropriate for a Christian. The temple prostitutes were real people, even if the gods being worshiped were not real gods. He decisively put an end to any notion that a person could engage in sexual immorality and consider it acceptable before the Lord Jesus Christ.

These details relate to the passage of Scripture noted above, but I want you to understand these points:

First, Paul made it clear that the body is the temple of the Holy Spirit. You live in your body, but you are more than flesh and bones. The inner self— soul and spirit—lives on after the physical body dies. While believers live on this earth as His creations, our bodies are simultaneously indwelled by the Holy Spirit. You are not only a vessel for your soul and spirit but also for the Spirit's presence and power. In this way, your physical self is a holy entity, devoted to worship. Your body is a temple of God's presence. Paul's ringing message throughout all of his writings is this: I am in Christ, and Christ is in me.

Second, given that the Holy Spirit has made you His temple on earth, you are to "glorify God" in your body and in your spirit. You should treat your physical being with the same respect you have for your eternal spirit.

The Greeks and Romans were known for the elaborate beauty and grandeur of their temples. Paul did not teach that we are to spend inordinate time, effort, or money on making our bodies beautiful. Rather, he called people to modesty. His emphasis was always on inner beauty and character. Paul was more concerned about the function of the temple in which we live, not the appearance of it. His admonitions were primarily about behavior.

According to Paul, each of us has a responsibility as a Christian to make certain that behaviors associated with our physical bodies bring honor to God. In writing to the Galatians, the apostle identified a number of "works of the flesh" that Christians should avoid: "adultery, fornication, uncleanness, lewdness [sensuality], idolatry, sorcery, hatred, contentions, jealousies, outbursts of wrath, selfish ambitions, dissensions [disputes for the sake of arguing], heresies, envy, murders, drunkenness, revelries," and other similar negative behaviors. Paul stated in no uncertain terms, "Those who practice such things will not inherit the kingdom of God" (Gal. 5:19–21).

Paul wrote equally strong words in his first letter to the Corinthians:

> Do not be deceived. Neither fornicators, nor idolaters, nor adulterers, nor homosexuals, nor sodomites, nor thieves, nor covetous, nor drunkards, nor revilers, nor extortioners will inherit the kingdom of God. And such were some of you. But you were washed, but you were sanctified, but you were justified in the name of the Lord Jesus and by the Spirit of our God. (6:9–11)

This passage is very important for us to understand. Paul was blunt in writing that our behavior is subject to our will. You and I choose how we will behave. What goes on in our bodies, how we use our bodies, and how we behave in our bodies are matters of our choosing.

"But," some people argue, "I'm just made a certain way. I can't help sinning."

My response to you is, "Oh yes, you can!"

You may not be able to keep from being tempted. Every person is at some point in life. You may have an ungodly desire that you have not fully submitted to Christ's redemptive power. But you do not need to sin. You do not need to act on every impulse you feel—whether it is a sexual desire, a craving for a particular food, a longing for a cigarette, or a passion for an alcoholic beverage. You have been given the ability, by the power of the Holy Spirit within you, to say no to any behavior that is insulting, detrimental, sullying, or damaging to your relationship with God and your testimony before other people.

Paul said that you have been washed—you have been cleansed from sin and forgiven by Christ Jesus. You have been sanctified—set apart for holy living, which is pure living outside the sin of the world. You have been justified—brought into alignment and intimacy with God. Believers are called to evaluate our behavior against the template of His purity.

What you do with your body is an act of praise to God. Therefore, anything you do to hurt or damage your body will prevent or limit you from fully honoring the Lord and making yourself freely available for service to Him.

GOD'S OWNERSHIP RIGHTS

I cringe when I hear people say, "My body is my body. I can do what I want with it." That's not what God's Word says!

Let's be clear that the Bible does not accept violence, abuse, or rape to any degree. No one has a right to violate another person's body or to inflict pain upon another individual. There is no justification for physical assault.

But it is equally true that you do not have a right to do anything you want with your body. You do not have a right to hurt yourself. Just as no other person has a right to abuse your body, you do not have a right to abuse yourself!

Furthermore, a pregnant woman does not have a right to assault or abuse the unborn child growing within her. That baby is not an extension of the mother's body. That little boy or girl is growing inside her, connected by a nutrient- and oxygen-transporting umbilical cord. That baby is not part of the mother's tissue. He or she is a person—an individual with a unique genetic code and a completely separate identity established at the moment of conception.

Assault, abuse, and violence are wrong. They are wrong behaviors from adult to adult, child to child, adult to child, child to adult, and mother to fetus. It is also wrong for you to commit assault, abuse, and violence against yourself!

And don't be fooled—sin always has consequences. The evil we commit against our bodies is the reason for countless types of diseases. The wrong behaviors we engage in using our bodies also produce damaging results. And understand this: "The wages of sin is death" (Rom. 6:23).

The consequences of sin put us on a path toward death. We may not die immediately, but the trend is set. The initial symptoms may be minor. But over time, if sin takes root and becomes habitual, the symptoms will become more obvious and severe.

If you are reading this as a parent, you need to teach your child that he does not have a right to put certain substances into his body, to pour alcohol into his body, to engage in sex before marriage, to inject drugs, to inhale damaging chemicals or addictive substances (including nicotine in all its forms). Why not? Because your child's body is a gift from God and it belongs to Him! God holds the Maker's Certificate for your body and for every other body He has ever created.

You do not have a right, even if the government gives you the right or if your friends and family members give you the right. That does not matter to God. The Lord has not given you the right to assault, abuse, or violate your body.

A friend of mine was stopped a few years ago by a policeman who asked to see not only her driver's license, but also the vehicle's proof of ownership. The interesting thing is that she was not violating any traffic laws in her driving. This policeman had pulled up behind her and noticed that the tag on her car had expired.

Well, she looked in the place where she always kept the registration and ownership papers, but she didn't find them. The fact was, she had owned the car for less than a year and thought the ownership had been transferred to her by the dealer. But it had not. The policeman accessed state records and found that her car was still rightfully owned by someone else. Fortunately for her, the officer gave her verbal advice about how to get the ownership transferred the next day rather than arrest her for possession of a stolen car!

That experience startled her to say the least. She told me, "I had no way of proving that the car I was driving was mine. It suddenly hit me— there really is no proof that anything I own, or even the body in which I live, is really mine. All things come from God and belong to Him. He just gives us occupancy rights and driving privileges."

Catch hold of that truth. God holds the "ownership papers" on your body. The Lord allows you to live in your body just as if He was the owner of an automobile He allowed you to drive. Treat what God has loaned you with respect, and use it with wisdom. Take care of what He has entrusted to you.

YOU HAVE STEWARDSHIP RESPONSIBILITY

God is the Owner of all the earth's property, including the earthen vessel in which you live. Your role is stewardship. You are responsible for temple upkeep. You bear responsibility for doing all that you can do to ensure that your body is given the right nutrients, kept in the best shape, and is full of energy. You need to be physically prepared and available for whatever form of service the Lord asks you to undertake.

Imagine for a moment a person who allows every drinking glass in his home to become dirty—not just a little dusty, but grimy, filthy, and filled with the residue of various prior beverages. A thirsty person comes to the door, and the Lord speaks to the heart of the home owner: *I want you to give a cup of cold water to this person in My name.*

Before that can happen, the embarrassed home owner must wash a glass and then fill it with pure water. By that time, the thirsty visitor may very well have gone next door. An opportunity for genuine service and its resulting reward from God have been missed.

If you allow your body to become sluggish, polluted, infected, or weak, instead of keeping it active, cleansed, strong, and protected, you will miss out on exciting, potential-fulfilling opportunities to serve others and bring glory to God.

Now I know that not all diseases or accidents can be avoided. I am aware that not everybody is born with a healthy body or one capable of all normal functions. Even so, every person can do a great deal to achieve health and maintain it.

This does not mean that you need to spend hours every day working out at a gym to build massive muscles. And you don't need to be preoccupied with matters related to how you feel, how you look, or what you are capable or incapable of doing. Most people already spend too much time thinking about their appearance. God's balance is this: we need to spend the right amount of time pursuing health and fitness so we can live to the maximum of our physical potential.

Because part of your potential lies in the function of your spirit, you must seek always to have a clean heart. Because part of your potential lies in the function of your mind, you must seek always to have pure thoughts. And because part of your potential lies in the use of your God-given natural and motivational gifts, you must seek out both instruction and experiences that develop them. In much the same way, part of your potential lies in the full function of your body.

God calls each of us to have:

- A clean body
- A fully functioning body
- A strong body
- A healthy body

And then He calls us to use our bodies in ways that retain purity, health, energy, and strength.

A Clean Body

We've all heard the statement, "You are what you eat." It also applies to what we drink, what we inhale, and what we touch. God desires that you take into your body only what is pure and nutritious. That means clean air, clean water, and healthful foods and beverages. God desires that you guard what comes in contact with your skin, and that you regularly bathe your body. God desires that you make your immediate environment as healthful as possible—which includes keeping your home free from impurities and harmful chemicals.

A Fully Functioning Body

A fully functioning body has both energy and flexibility. For your body to have energy, you need to eat the right foods, stay physically active, and get sufficient sleep.

One of the most important systems within your body is the lymphatic system. It works and secretes immunity-related hormones only when the body is in motion. Regardless of your physical state, keep moving! Exercise whatever you are capable of moving, and choose to remain as flexible and active as you can.

A Strong Body

A strong body has the endurance and ability to perform physical tasks to their completion. Strength comes from weight-bearing or resistance exercises. Medical researchers have discovered that even people who use wheelchairs can do exercises to build various muscle groups in their bodies

The health of your muscles is not only related to strength; the energy stored in your cells governs the metabolism of your body and regulates the storage of fat in your tissues. Choose to do exercises that strengthen your muscles.

The heart, of course, is a muscle. Aerobic exercise strengthens the heart and the entire cardiovascular system. Walking, jogging, swimming and a host of other activities will help keep your heart strong and your blood vessels clear.

A Healthy Body

A healthy body is free of disease and infection. Two of the easiest things you can do are also the most effective. The first is to wash your hands regularly for a sufficient length of time to kill germs. (Experts say that singing the "Happy Birthday" song twice will allow enough time for soap to thoroughly cleanse your skin.) The second is to avoid touching any part of your face with your fingers. Most people are surprised by how often they bring their fingers to their mouths and noses in the course of a day. It is an automatic impulse for most people.

If you have a weak or compromised immune system, stay away from large crowds during cold and flu season. Watch what you touch in public places.

All of these are very simple and practical suggestions.

The obvious bottom-line question is this, "Would you rather be sick or well?" I don't know anybody who would choose weakness, illness, disease, and frailty over strength, health, vitality, and energy!

GOD VALUES THE BODY

God has placed great value on our bodies. In the first place, He chose to create man as a physical being. The Bible tells us that "the LORD God formed man of the dust of the ground, and breathed into his nostrils the breath of life; and man became a living being" (Gen. 2:7). Perhaps the most compelling evidence that affirms the value of the human body is the fact that Jesus took on flesh and became man. The incarnation—the indwelling of flesh by God—should send a message to each of us that our heavenly Father considers the physical body to be a vessel worthy of His presence.

It also is a message assuring us that Christ knew what it was like to feel pain and weakness.

Jesus certainly used His body in beneficial ways, perhaps most notably, touching those who were sick and making them well. The Son of Man valued health and wholeness. He knew that a person's physical health is a vital aspect of his or her overall life, and that without health, life is limited.

Jesus held little children in His arms, ate real food, and walked up and down the dusty roads of Israel in a real body. He bowed His knee to the Father in prayer and spoke with a real voice. Christ no doubt made real hand and facial gestures to crowds of people who came to hear Him preach and teach. He allowed Himself to be jostled by crowds of people. And Jesus moved in a physical body through a crowd of angry critics who sought to push Him off a cliff in His hometown of Nazareth.

In the last hours before His death on a cross, Jesus bore all of the marks of pain and suffering that can be inflicted upon a human body. His agony in the Garden of Gethsemane was so intense that blood and sweat poured from His real body. Fists and possibly rods were used by angry Jewish leaders to pummel His body in a rigged, late-night trial. A crown of thorns was crushed into His skull, and the whips of Rome scourged His body, ripping His skin and tearing His flesh. He staggered in a real body through the streets of Jerusalem to be mocked. His closest friends could scarcely recognize Him due to the gaping, swollen wounds and flowing blood that came from a very real physical body. Jesus died a physical death in a physical body, and His body, not only His spirit, was raised at the resurrection.

Does God understand what goes on in your body? Absolutely.

Does He know the limits of what you can withstand physically? Yes, indeed. Does God know how to heal whatever is wrong with your body? Oh, yes.

Does He know what it feels like to die? Yes, He does.

Does God understand physical impulses to sin? The Bible tells us that Jesus was tempted in every way that human beings are tempted, yet He did not sin. Christ knew physical temptation. The Lord understands how difficult it is to say no to the lusts of the flesh.

Holy, pure, and sinless God was willing to live within a physical body to show us that it is possible to live a holy, pure, and sin-overcoming life as human beings.

WHAT ABOUT PEOPLE
WITH PHYSICAL LIMITATIONS?

You may ask, "But what about the person who is born with a difficult physical condition or ailment? What about someone who contracts a terrible illness or has a horrible accident? Isn't it impossible for those people to pursue and reach their full potential?" No. It is entirely possible.

In fact, some people reach their full potential and accomplish God's purpose for them only as a result of hardships, difficulties, and tragedies in their lives or in their health. For the most part, however, that is not the way life works. Most of us have the challenge of pursuing and maintaining a healthy body so we can fulfill our potential and our purpose. Good health is necessary to be and do all that God has for us to be and do.

I do not in any way dismiss or diminish the power of a sick or disabled person to influence his world. Years ago, I received regular and ongoing encouragement from a man who had once been a pastor and who has since gone home to be with the Lord. He battled illness for many years. And by the time I met him, he was confined to his bed with a degenerative disease. Even so, he called me as many as three or four times a week. He'd ask me in a very weak and faltering voice, "What can I pray about?" He routinely asked about the needs in my life. I'd give him an answer, and he'd take that to heart, hang up, and go to prayer on my behalf and on behalf of others in my church. On Saturday evenings, he often called to ask me what I was planning to preach and how I was feeling about my sermon. He'd ask me to give him a specific prayer assignment, and I did.

I cannot begin to calculate the influence he had on my life, on my ministry, and on my church during the years we were in regular contact. Only eternity will reveal the fullness of his ministry, even within a weakened and declining physical state.

Having said all that, let me add something: This man was in communication with me and knew how best to direct his prayers because he dialed a phone with his physical body and talked to me with a physical voice. There wasn't a lot he could do physically, but he used what strength and ability he did have to make a difference in my life. I could feel his faith over the phone. I knew he was making a very real impact in the spiritual realm as he prayed with the lungs, vocal cords, and mouth of his physical body.

The apostle Paul wrote from a prison cell these words to the Philippians:

> I considered it necessary to send to you Epaphroditus, my brother, fellow worker, and fellow soldier, but your messenger and the one who ministered to my need; since he was longing for you all, and was distressed because you had heard that he was sick. For indeed he was sick

almost unto death; but God had mercy on him, and not only on him but on me also, lest I should have sorrow upon sorrow. (Phil. 2:25–27)

Note that sentence, "God had mercy on him." God did not send the sickness. We live in a fallen world, and the devil takes full advantage of that. God has *mercy* on the sick. All healing is an act of mercy.

The healing was for both Epaphroditus, who was healed in his body, and Paul. The apostle received emotional relief from his deep concern for his friend and was spared "sorrow upon sorrow" should Epaphroditus have died.

The mercy of God was extended to Epaphroditus so he could return to Philippi with Paul's letter to the church there. I have absolutely no doubt that a big reason for Epaphroditus' healing was so he might be a messenger between the Philippians and Paul. He brought things that allowed the apostle to live a tolerable life under Roman prison conditions, then took Paul's letter back to the church at Philippi. Without the successful mission of Epaphroditus, we might not have the book of Philippians—one of the most encouraging, inspiring, and instructive books in the New Testament. What a loss that would have been to the church for the last two thousand years. We need to praise God for allowing Epaphroditus to deliver that scroll to the believers in Philippi!

NO IMMUNITY FROM LIFE'S CIRCUMSTANCES

Each of us lives in a fallen world. God's people are not immune from tragedy or sickness. Through the years, I have known many wonderful Christian men and women who have suffered terribly. I do not have an adequate explanation for why God allows some of the best and brightest saints on this earth to suffer with illness or to be maimed in an accident. What I do know is this:

God never stops loving the people, nor does He stop extending His mercy to them.

The Lord has purposes that we will never understand, and He uses all things to fulfill His greater purpose, not only in the lives of the suffering people but in the lives of those around them.

Potential is not cut off in times of a tragedy or sickness; rather, it is redirected. Think of the athlete who has an accident or is diagnosed with an illness that suddenly and completely ends his potential to play a particular sport. There are numerous examples of athletes who, as committed Christians, redirected their focus and their energies toward a new pursuit. And what they accomplished as witnesses for Jesus Christ after their athletic careers ended was greater than what they accomplished before.

Potential does not end with the diagnosis of a serious disease or condition. It continues—but perhaps in a new direction.

Our concern should not be how an accident or illness occurs. Nor should we wonder how God will choose to show mercy to His beloved children who suffer through them. Our concern should be avoiding accidents and illnesses that can be avoided. There is a great deal we can do to remain healthy, and there simply is no excuse for neglecting to care for our physical bodies.

EDUCATE YOURSELF ABOUT YOUR BODY

Part of having a healthy body is related to knowing how your body functions and how to take care of it. Many people have never learned how to eat right. Nutritious foods provide essential vitamins and minerals to the body. A nutritious diet includes eating healthy foods that refuel, repair, and rejuvenate, without adding elements that weaken or compromise the body.

I have been amazed through the years to meet people who are highly educated and intelligent in many respects, yet they know very little about how their bodies function or what their bodies need. People rarely know the side effects associated with their prescribed medications. Most do not seem to understand the dangers associated with various chemicals. And many who are under thirty years of age seem to have a remarkable (and unfounded) sense of invincibility that I once encountered only in teenagers. They mistakenly think, *It can't happen to me,* when it comes to all kinds of degenerative diseases.

If you don't know the basics of good nutrition, the value of different kinds of exercises, or the importance of lifestyle factors in avoiding major diseases, I strongly encourage you to seek out that information immediately.

I also encourage you to:

1. Learn the basics of good nutrition.
2. Learn about different kinds of exercise and their respective benefits to your physical well-being, and find out how to safely and correctly do the exercises that may be recommended for you.
3. Ask questions about any substance that is recommended to you for an ongoing condition. Know the downside of various medications and the risks involved. The same goes for herbal and natural medical remedies and nutritional supplements. (Never lose sight of the fact that a snake bite is "natural," but it is not likely to be beneficial.)
4. Take the supplements and medications that you need for better health. But take your medications only *as prescribed.* Don't overtake them, and don't take medications on a hit-or-miss basis.
5. Monitor various vital signs and health indicators on a routine basis—including your blood pressure, lung capacity, blood-sugar levels, weight, cholesterol, and various hormone levels. See a doctor annually for physical examinations and advice.
6. Get a second opinion if a major surgery or course of treatment is recommended to you for a particular disease or condition.

7. Understand that not all medications work in the same way in every person's body. Also be aware that while your nutritional needs are similar to those of the population as a whole, some of your requirements are likely to be unique to you as an individual. Work with experts in nutrition to plan your diet.

8. Recognize that you bear the final responsibility for your health.

9. Stop harmful habits. If you need to detox your body, get the help you need. If you need to overcome an addiction, seek wise counsel and face up to your problem.

10. Recognize that prevention beats a cure any day.

I also strongly urge you never to discount the power of God to heal. Our heavenly Father not only can cure all manner of sickness and disease, but He has healed and does heal people of countless ailments that are supposedly incurable.

Pray for your health, and ask others who believe in the healing power of God to pray for you. Ask the Lord to increase your faith, just as the father of a terribly afflicted boy once said to Jesus, "Lord, I believe; help my unbelief" (Mark 9:24).

DOMINION OVER
A PHYSICAL WORLD

Part of the reason you need to live in the healthiest body possible is that God's challenge to all of humanity is to take dominion over a physical world. The Lord said at the time He created man, "Let Us make man in Our image, according to Our likeness; let them have dominion over the fish of the sea, over the birds of the air, and over the cattle, over all the earth and over every creeping thing that creeps on the earth" (Gen. 1:26).

God gave mankind the awesome responsibility to take care of the earth, along with our physical bodies. The way you take care of your body and the world around you contributes—negatively or positively—in a small way toward the care of humanity and the environment as a whole.

A major part of your stewardship—and of your dominion over the physical world—is the challenge of defeating the enemies of your earthly body.

THE ENEMIES OF THE HUMAN BODY

Without a doubt, some specific substances are enemies of your body. They do not promote health. Instead, they inflict physical damage on the cells and tissues of the body. These substances also generate the potential for suffering and injury. Here are four colossal enemies of your body:

1. Alcohol

Some people tell me that they "only" drink beer—as if it doesn't have alcohol in it. Other people tell me that they've heard that a glass of wine is good for the body. A substance in red wine that may be helpful is called resveratrol. But a person would have to drink dozens of glasses of wine a day to gain its benefits. If you want to take resveratrol, you can purchase little capsules that go down easily and don't produce a state of drunkenness or lead to alcoholism. Alcohol destroys brain cells, and too much of it over time can destroy liver cells to the point of this vital organ's failure. Alcohol in varying quantities clouds a person's thinking and robs him of physical coordination.

Another problem with alcohol is that you don't know how much your body can tolerate unless you drink it. That's a dangerous proposition. Also, you don't know how much alcohol will push you over the line into addiction. For some people, it's only one drink!

I can't even begin to tell you all the other problems that alcohol is linked to besides a person's health. From drunk-driving accidents to family breakups to job loss, the list goes on and on.

2. Tobacco

Cigarettes, cigars, pipes, and chewing tobacco provide no health benefits. The lungs are polluted if tobacco is smoked, and the tissues of the digestive tract are compromised if tobacco is chewed or swallowed.

"But it helps me relax," some people say. "It helps keep me thin" is another excuse. God has many ways to help you relax and control your weight that don't turn the inside of your body black from tar and put you at risk for some of the most devastating diseases known to man.

3. Drugs

There is no health benefit from using any drug that becomes addictive and requires you to use more and more of it to get less and less benefit. Whether a person abuses prescription medication or illegal substances, such as marijuana and cocaine, drug addiction is physically, emotionally, mentally, and spiritually devastating. Don't start and you'll spare yourself the problems associated with stopping.

Some people claim that drugs make them more energetic or more relaxed, which allows them to work better and relate to others more freely. The truth is that drugs destroy far more than they enhance. If taken regularly and long enough, they will destroy the tissues of your brain and body, impair your ability to think, create, and function, and tear down the very relationships you were so eager to build.

The big lie about alcohol, tobacco, and drug use is that popular people are doing it; therefore, everybody should. In truth, the so-called popular people associated with these substances very often end up in expensive rehab facilities. They struggle for a significant portion of their careers with remaining sober enough to do the work that created their popularity. Alcohol is a multi-billion-dollar industry. The same goes for tobacco. There's no calculating how much money changes hands with illegal drugs. But the overuse of prescription medications totals into the billions of dollars. Commercials promote the use of alcohol. Movies and television glamorize drug use, and too few people rise up and call for an end to it. Illegal drug use is abuse of the body in the rawest, most devastating, and most easily preventable form.

4. Sexually Transmitted Diseases

Virtually no diseases are linked directly to monogamous sex within marriage. Yet countless diseases are associated with sexual promiscuity, whether heterosexual or homosexual. Sexually transmitted diseases are increasing in number, not decreasing, despite billions of dollars spent on messages calling for people to practice "safe sex." The only truly safe sex is within a monogamous, heterosexual marriage—that is, the faithful marriage between a man and a woman.

Perhaps no message in our nation is more politically incorrect at the moment than this one. But look at the statistics related to these diseases, the death rates in various nations around the world, the rising amounts of people suffering from emotional trauma associated with sex-related diseases, and the increasing number of orphans worldwide. God has a wonderful plan for sex, yet man willfully chooses to violate that plan. I don't care what kind of fantasies or tendencies you think you were born with. Engaging in sex is an act of your willful behavior, unless you are violated in some way. Choose to have sex in the way that is not contrary to God's commandments.

The Consequences

In our nation alone, two trillion dollars are spent each year on health care to deal with diseases associated with these four enemies of the human body—all of which are preventable. That amount of money should make most people's head spin. I have no doubt that if two trillion dollars were made available to me, I could get the gospel of Jesus Christ into the hands of every person on this planet!

We spend money to get sick, and then we spend even more money to try to get well.

The dollar figure is staggering, but so are the numbers in terms of pain, suffering, and death. Entire areas of Africa have lost almost the entire adult population because of sexually transmitted diseases, the vast majority of which have no known cure.

If you don't hear it from anybody else, hear it from me.

Don't use alcohol.

Don't inhale or chew tobacco in any form.

Don't use illegal drugs or overuse prescription medications.

Don't engage in sexual activity outside of heterosexual marriage.

It's not my plan for better health. It's God's plan.

THE ENEMY OF STRESS

Stress is just as potent an enemy of the human body as any of the four behaviors identified above. But it is not related to a particular substance and is secondary to a wide variety of emotional and psychological responses to life. The emotions or situations very often linked to stress include ongoing and unresolved:

- hatred;
- bitterness;
- anger;
- resentment;
- worry, anxiety, and frustration;
- discouragement, often related to feelings of low self-value or low self-worth;
- grief;
- failure;

- overindulgence in any area of life, including overworking and overeating;
- loss, including job loss or loss of a loving relationship.

What stresses you may not stress another person. Stress is highly individualized. Yet research reveals that while it is linked to many diseases, stress also relates to the rate at which people heal or recover from accidents and injuries. It either causes or is the result of family discord and failure at work. It is linked to addiction, depression, and feelings of despair that can lead to suicide.

Entire books have been written about stress, and there isn't space here to go into the subject in more depth. But let me remind you of this: God's Word addresses every human response that has been linked to stress. Scripture is full of strong admonitions about laying aside anger and hatred. The Bible tells us not to be anxious about anything. God's Word says we need to live a balanced life, to trust the Lord in all situations, and to not let resentment and bitterness take root in our lives.

Go to God with the factors that are causing you to feel stressed. Talk it over with your Maker. Go to His Word and study the passages related to what's causing your stress. Study the examples in the Bible of people who dealt with those things successfully, and take warning from those who didn't.

Often overlooked in discussions about health is the difference that a faith-filled, positive attitude can have on a person. Extending the number of days that God has allotted to us is not the issue. It's the impact that faith and a positive attitude have on a person's quality of life. I have watched people who were negative toward life and toward their bodies act very old, even when they were in their fifties and sixties. On the other hand, I know numerous people who are very positive toward life, and they are "young" even in their nineties.

Those who trust God, the Bible says, will renew their strength and soar like an eagle—at any age. Those who trust God are empowered by Him to run without being weary and to walk without fainting (Isa. 40:31).

Trust God with your health and with your life. He can help you overcome any thing that causes stress.

OTHERS SOURCES OF STRESS ON THE HUMAN BODY

In addition to psychological and emotional factors, environmental pollution can also create stress. Some of these pollutants actually change the size and function of cells. Others set up a chain reaction that causes oxidation in our bodies. This process is the same one that causes a banana to turn brown when it is exposed to air.

Pollutants can suffocate the tissues of the lungs. They can contribute to increased infection in the body.

Bacteria, viruses, and fungi can invade your body and add to stress.

The good news is that all forms of stress have a God solution.

The key is to take the time and make the effort to discover what may be keeping you from the best health possible. If stress factors are involved, pray that the Lord will show you what is happening and lead you to information to help you overcome them. If your behavior needs to change, ask God to help you desire His will more than your own.

WHY DON'T WE TAKE BETTER CARE OF OUR BODIES?

Ask yourself, "Am I truly taking the best possible care of my body?" If not, what is my excuse for failing to take care of it?

People do not take proper care of their bodies for a number of reasons. But I believe there are two primary causes which stand out from the rest.

First, many people don't believe the consequences of poor health habits will affect them. They think that somehow, and for some unknown reason, they are and will continue to be immune from the consequences associated with a poor diet or lack of exercise.

Second, many people who abuse their bodies or are bad stewards of what God has given them actually like their bad health habits. Everyone wants to feel good, but a lot of food, drink, and other things with a "feel-good" quality are not necessarily good for us. If we get a temporary high or a "lift" from a particular substance or behavior, we're likely to think that two of that is better than one.

And there's a reason certain foods are called comfort foods. Their high fat content gives us a sleepy, satisfied feeling. Think about the so-called comfort foods you enjoy. In all likelihood, they are loaded with fat.

Then there are the pick-me-up foods and beverages. Their high sugar content revs up the metabolism temporarily, creating a brief feeling of energy. And once it wears off, many people experience a "crash" and are worse off than they were before.

Too much fat and sugar significantly and negatively affects your health. The short-term "benefits" can have terrible, long-term consequences.

CHECK YOUR ATTITUDE
ABOUT HEALTH

Check your attitude today.

How do you feel about your body?

How do you feel about caring for your body?

What is your attitude toward health?

Who owns your body?

How do feel about God's ownership of your body?

What is your attitude toward good nutrition?

What is your attitude toward exercise?

The way you think about your health and staying physically fit will impact the pursuit of your God-given potential!

A LIFE OF POTENTIAL PURSUED

DANIEL

Everyone said that Daniel was an up-and-comer. He was bright and personable, and he loved God. Nobody was surprised when he landed a good-paying job straight out of college.

Through the years, Daniel was given promotion after promotion. Along with the increased responsibility in his work came increased pressure to perform. His work days often extended into the night. His business trips became more frequent and more intense.

Many of Daniel's clients and business associates were heavy drinkers, and a great many business deals were discussed or closed over dinners that included alcoholic beverages. Before long, Daniel was having drinks before dinner, during dinner, and after dinner—at least three or four nights a week.

While Daniel liked how the alcohol helped him relax, he did not like the morning headache that came after a long business dinner the night before.

As the pressures to perform mounted during tough economic times in his business sector, Daniel talked to a friend who was a psychologist. The friend recommended a particular medication to Daniel to help him with anxiety and sleep. He advised Daniel to take it only when he felt especially anxious. He warned that the medication could become addictive.

This anxiety and sleep aid really worked for Daniel. And from his perspective, if one pill was good, two would probably be better. So he took more and more of the medication, and when he ran out of pills, he told his psychologist friend that he was having panic attacks that probably called for his taking more of it.

Before long Daniel was addicted to both the alcohol and the prescription medication. And to seriously complicate matters, he was mixing his drinking with his pill taking, even though the warning label for the medication clearly stated that a person taking it regularly should not consume alcohol.

The day came when Daniel went berserk. There's no other way to describe what happened. He showed up at work wearing mismatched clothes and talking gibberish. He was immediately transported to a hospital, and within hours, he was in intensive care being treated for what amounted to brain-tissue poisoning. It took weeks for Daniel to recover physically. His treatment included spending two weeks in another hospital for emotional and psychological counseling.

Daniel came out of that experience seriously questioning his faith, his relationship with God, his goals in life, and the kind of lifestyle he wanted to have.

He said to an associate pastor at his church, "I let God down. I'm wondering if I was ever in the right line of work." The pastor prayed with Daniel, who was quick to seek the Lord's forgiveness. Then he asked if God ever provided any input into what line of work was right for Daniel. "Not really. I just took the first high-paying job that was offered to me," Daniel replied

"Have you ever given any thought to what you would really like to do if you could have any job you wanted?" the pastor asked.

Daniel smiled and, after a moment or two, said, "I'd really like to work outdoors with my hands."

"Then do it," the pastor said before praying that God would lead Daniel to the right opportunity and give him a ministry within his new job.

That's exactly what happened. Daniel began to work for the U.S. Forest Service, and he continues in that job today. At times, the work is backbreaking—clearing rock slides and clogged river channels. Other times, the work includes firefighting and challenging search-and-rescue work locating missing hikers. Best of all, Daniel feels no need to drink or use anti-anxiety medication. And there's no major stress to take home at the end of the day.

Daniel's new job also allowed him to have time for a social life. He met a young woman who shared his goals, and they married after a couple years of dating. Both became actively involved in the youth ministry at their church. Daniel had always enjoyed singing, although he had never done very much of it. His wife has an outstanding voice and is an accomplished pianist. Together, they work with the teenagers in their church to host a series of summer concerts in the city where they live. Both see it as an evangelistic outreach and as an opportunity to showcase the talent in their church.

Is Daniel pursuing his God-given potential?

Without a doubt.

CHAPTER 8

ESSENTIAL #5:
RIGHT RELATIONSHIPS

Is your life rich with friendships?

Do you feel loved, appreciated, and valued by others?

Or do you feel alone or in conflict with people?

Do you have healthy give-and-take relationships?

Are your relationships satisfying and challenging to you?

As you follow the path toward fulfilling your God-given potential, you will discover rather quickly that you do not walk it alone. You will not arrive at the fullness of your potential without getting and giving help along the way.

No one lives in isolation. All of us have and need relationships.

They determine to a great extent how successful and joyful we are. Our relationships make it possible for us to pursue various goals and engage in various activities. And they play a key role in helping us overcome adversities and hardships.

All of the previous topics we have covered—a clean heart, a clear mind, a set of gifts and talents, and a healthy body—relate to the way you interact with people. The lives of others, in turn, impact your understanding of what it means to live in a forgiven, intimate, pure relationship with God and His children. Through our relationships we learn what it means to have a clear mind, what it means to have and use your natural and ministry-motivated gifts, and what it means to live in as much health and vitality as you can.

God's Word tells us about the early church in Antioch:

> Now in the church that was at Antioch there were certain prophets and teachers: Barnabas, Simeon who was called Niger, Lucius of Cyrene, Manaen who had been brought up with Herod the tetrarch, and Saul. As they ministered to the Lord and fasted, the Holy Spirit said, "Now separate to Me Barnabas and Saul for the work to which I have called them." Then, having fasted and prayed, and laid hands on them, they sent them away.
>
> So, being sent out by the Holy Spirit, they went down to Seleucia, and from there they sailed to Cyprus. And when they arrived in Salamis, they preached the word of God in the synagogues of the Jews. They also had John as their assistant (Acts 13:1–5).

I want to point out to you two things about this brief passage. First, the church sent out a team of two people who were expected to minister together with complementary talents and abilities. On at least two occasions in His ministry, Jesus had sent out His closest disciples two by two (Mark 6:7, Luke 10:1). The early church knew the success of this model. Two people who are in agreement about the gospel and who are working together as a close-knit team can do more than two isolated individuals functioning totally on their own.

Although this particular trip is often called Paul's First Missionary

Journey, the apostle was not sent out alone. In fact, since the name of Barnabas comes first, this church may have regarded him as the leader of this two-man team. Barnabas had been part of the body of believers in Jerusalem from very early in its founding, perhaps from the day of Pentecost when that church was birthed in both the natural and the spiritual realms. At one point Barnabas sought out Paul to bring him to Jerusalem so the church could validate his conversion and leadership. Barnabas is the name that the apostles gave to him. His real name was Joses, but he was called Barnabas because the name means "Son of Encouragement." That tells you a lot about who he was in terms of personality and ministry gifting.

Paul was an exhorter, a strong preacher, a brilliant Bible scholar, and a no-nonsense man who had a powerful and dynamic way of presenting the gospel. Barnabas was very likely more of a people person, helping primarily with the gift of mercy, and perhaps with giving and administration. He was one of those who sold land and brought all of the money to help support the first believers in Jerusalem—he knew about financial matters and was generous in giving.

Second, the church authorized only two people to go on this trip: Barnabas and Paul. These two men had been separated for the work, had received the prayers of the believers in Antioch, and had hands laid upon them to authorize them spiritually for their journey.

But for whatever reasons may have seemed good at the time, Barnabas and Paul took along a young man named John as their assistant. He was John Mark, who is credited with later writing the gospel of Mark. John Mark was Barnabas's cousin. Later in Acts, we read what happened on their trip:

> Paul said to Barnabas, "Let us now go back and visit our brethren in every city where we have preached the word of the Lord, and see how they are doing." Now Barnabas was determined to take with them John

called Mark. But Paul insisted that they should not take with them the one who had departed from them in Pamphylia, and had not gone with them to the work. Then the contention became so sharp that they parted from one another. And so Barnabas took Mark and sailed to Cyprus; but Paul chose Silas and departed, being commended by the brethren to the grace of God. And he went through Syria and Cilicia, strengthening the churches. (Acts 15:36–41)

John Mark had bailed out of the mission before it was completed. He had deserted Barnabas and Paul before the trip was over and the mission was fulfilled. Again, we do not know all the reasons, but the reasons were strong enough and important enough to Paul that he was determined not to go on another mission trip with John Mark. Barnabas was equally determined that John Mark be given a second chance. Again, you can see the difference in personality of these two leaders and the ways in which these differences relate to their respective ministry gifts.

In the end, Paul and Silas went one way, and Barnabas and Mark, another.

Two men who ministered together in a powerful way and forged a very strong bond of friendship had a disagreement that separated them for a great while.

We don't know much about the ministry of Barnabas after that separation. He is mentioned in other places in the New Testament—but always in association with Paul. They apparently mended any hard feelings between them.

Later, we read about this in Paul's letter to Timothy, a young man whom the apostle had mentored for ministry. He wrote, "Get Mark and bring him with you, for he is useful to me for ministry" (2 Tim. 4:11).

Mark apparently had matured or had proven himself in subsequent ministry to the point that Paul considered him a man he wanted by his side and on his team once again.

We can learn several truths from this set of relationships:

1. God puts us in relationship for purposes of effective ministry and for mutual support as human beings.
2. The Lord wants us to be in relationship with people who are consistent and loyal—people who can be counted upon, regardless of situations and circumstances.
3. God expects us to forgive people who hurt us, but He does not require us to continue to trust people who abandon us. The Lord does not require us to continue working with people who are disloyal to us or behave in ways that are detrimental to our ministry efforts.
4. God wants us to be sensitive to the fact that everybody makes mistakes and has an opportunity to learn and grow from them. Each of us is under development, to some degree, all the days of our lives. If a person makes a mistake, we should consider giving him or her a second chance to do the right thing. Very often, those who continue in their error are people we should avoid.

Relationships are God's plan!

BIBLICAL EXAMPLES OF POSITIVE RELATIONSHIPS

The Bible is filled with stories of people who accomplished great things, but only because they were in relationship with others.

Noah didn't build the ark alone. He had three sons and their families to help him.

Moses worked as a team with various people in his leadership role of the Israelites. His brother, Aaron, was his spokesman as he went again and again to demand that Pharaoh let the Israelites leave Egypt. Moses learned from his father-in-law that he could not handle all the judicial matters of the Israelites on his own. He was given a template for sharing that dimension of leadership with proven elders. Moses worked with the leaders of each tribe in sending spies to check out the Promised Land.

Moses had a special relationship with Joshua. He led the children of Israel out of Egypt to the border of the Promised Land. Joshua led the children of Israel into the Promised Land and through the first phase of their conquest of it. Exodus 17 describes the events:

> Amalek came and fought with Israel in Rephidim. And Moses said to Joshua, "Choose us some men and go out, fight with Amalek. Tomorrow I will stand on the top of the hill with the rod of God in my hand." So Joshua did as Moses said to him and fought with Amalek. And Moses, Aaron and Hur went up to the top of the hill. And so it was, when Moses held up his hand, that Israel prevailed; and when he let down his hand, Amalek prevailed. But Moses' hands became heavy, so they took a stone and put it under him, and he sat on it. And Aaron and Hur supported his hands, one on one side, and the other on the other side, and his hands were steady until the going down of the sun. So Joshua defeated Amalek and his people with the edge of the sword. (vv. 8–13)

This battle was won with a four-man, team leadership effort. Joshua led the troops. Moses held the rod. And Aaron and Hur supported Moses, giving him strength and steadiness during the long battle. The victory that followed required the full participation of all four men. Each fulfilled a unique role, but all four worked together in relationship.

Nehemiah rebuilt the broken walls and gates of Jerusalem—but not by himself. He gathered a group of people and encouraged them to do the work. Nehemiah established such a strong relationship with the people in Jerusalem that they were willing to work with extreme diligence and effort. Each held a weapon in one hand, ready to defend the work, and a construction tool in the other hand (Neh. 4:17).

Even Jesus did not minister by Himself. He chose twelve men to surround and help Him in practical ways. One was chosen for the unique role of Christ's betrayer (Judas). Jesus developed such a strong bond with eleven of His apostles that every one of them was willing to die for his Lord and Savior. In fact, most of the apostles died a martyr's death. Jesus not only called them His disciples; He also called them friends.

Throughout his ministry, Paul had many associates. The Bible tells us about several of them—some are given only a brief mention. Apart from Barnabas and Silas, we know that Paul ministered actively with Timothy, Titus, Luke, Tychicus, Erastus, Trophimus, Miletus, Eubulus, Pudens, Linus, Claudia, and the household of Onesiphorus—all of whom helped Paul in some way for some purpose. He worked alongside Priscilla and Aquila in a tent-making business and also in building up the church in their city. He worked with Lydia to establish a church that met in her home. He no doubt worked closely with the apostle John for the two years that Paul had a teaching ministry in Ephesus. Paul called Mark, Aristarchus, Demas, and Epaphras his fellow laborers. He referred by name specifically to the work of, or his association with, Apphia, Archippus, Zenas, Apollos, Stephanas, Fortunatus, Achaicus, Philemon, Epaphras, and Onesimus.

God's plan is for you to be in relationships that provide mutual help and assistance. As much as you need other people for help and friendship, they need you for the same reasons.

I do not know the people whom God will call alongside you to help you reach your full potential, but I do know the characteristics of those you should choose for life's journey. These characteristics apply to your spouse as well as to your friends and business associates.

INSIGHTS INTO THE NATURE
OF RELATIONSHIPS

All relationships have ups and downs. We should never expect them to flow smoothly every hour of every day over the course of many years. Valuable relationships need to be nurtured and developed. Each person needs to be able to ride out times that are problematic and troublesome. That's part of the way God designed each person and relationship for growth.

All relationships are designed to embody a dual role of giving and receiving. If one person is doing all the giving and the other is doing all the receiving, there will be an imbalance.

All relationships enter times when the two people involved hurt each other—both intentionally and unintentionally. Therefore, every relationship is loaded with opportunities for forgiveness.

As problematic as they can be, relationships are God's plan for us. He does not want anyone to be alone. We are not to live in isolation, totally independent from all other people. We become who we are through our relationships with other people. You and I develop our character and are enriched and prepared for various tasks and experiences through our relationships.

God made us to have a relationship with Him and to be dependent on Him. But He also made us to have relationships with people and to be dependent—to some degree and in healthy ways—on them.

Look at the world around you.

No bridge of any size is built by just one person.

No skyscraper is built by just one person.

No house is built by just one person. Even if a person does build his home, he uses materials and furnishes it with items that other people have made.

No war is fought by just one soldier.

The biggest and best churches, businesses, and societies become that way because individuals and groups of people cooperate with one another.

HELPFUL OR DETRIMENTAL?

Every relationship in your life has a positive or negative effect. Because of that, you must seek God's wisdom about your relationships.

Recognize that you cannot and did not choose some relationships— your parents, grandparents, and others in your family tree, for example. You did not choose the culture and nation in which you were born. As a young child, you had no control over who your next-door neighbors would be. Therefore, you did not choose the playmates who were most accessible to you. If you were born into a Christian family, your parents chose the church where you first heard about Jesus.

Later in life, you made personal choices about most, if not all, of these relationships. You may have emigrated from your native land, adopted new cultural practices, chosen your neighbors, and selected your church or denomination. You may even have made a choice to distance yourself from various family members, especially if one or more of them were abusive to you. Even so, most of your early-life influencers were people you did not choose.

As an adult, you have a tremendous opportunity to make very clear and definite choices about the people you want in your life. You have or had the opportunity to choose a spouse. You and your spouse may have decided to have children. You have a choice about where you go to church, who your friends are, and with whom you participate in ministry activities. If you go to a large church, you may have a choice about which people are members of your small group. You also have opportunities to choose business associates, colleagues, mentors, counselors, teachers, students, and friends.

ESTABLISHING RIGHT RELATIONSHIPS

Some people do not seem to think it is necessary or even possible to make conscious choices about who they will have in their lives. I firmly believe that God wants you to have an active role in choosing the people in your life and, if you are a parent, choosing the people in your children's lives.

You need to have relationships with people who do the following:

- *Build your confidence*—both in God and in yourself. A good relationship bolsters your faith and your trust in the Lord. It builds you up—or edifies you—to believe for greater things and to pursue higher goals within the framework of an attitude that says "you can do it with God's help."
- *Encourage you in moments when you are discouraged.* The apostle Paul addressed these first two characteristics when he wrote to the church at Thessalonica, "Comfort each other and edify one another, just as you also are doing" (1 Thess. 5:11).
- *Motivate you to do your best.* Not everyone can be the winner. But we all can do our best, contribute the most we can contribute, and participate fully in building the morale of a team.
- *Stimulate you to greater creativity.* In good relationships, there is an exchange of new ideas and insights that give rise to new inventions, approaches, and perspectives.
- *Energize you.* How does a relationship energize? Joy is contagious; laughter is infectious. Joyful laughter sparks something inside us that spurs us on. Scientists say that laughter and joyful conversation spark the release of endorphins, "feel good" hormones released in the brain that are the body's natural painkillers. I can't tell you exactly what happens to a person physiologically, but I do know what God's Word says, "The joy of the LORD is your strength" (Neh. 8:10).

- *Comfort you when you are hurting.* Every person encounters pain in life, including the sting of rejection. A good relationship comforts you. It may come in the form of a listening ear, a shoulder to cry on, or even a gentle embrace. A true comforter is present in your hour of need.

- *Defend you when you are criticized or persecuted.* When your character is falsely attacked or your integrity is questioned, when your faith is challenged or your belief in Christ Jesus is ridiculed, there's nothing more helpful than someone who will stand up for you.

- *Forgive you when you make mistakes.* No one lives an error-free life. We all have faults and flaws, and we all falter and fail at times. You need to be in relationship with people who will forgive you quickly and freely, and then move forward. The best friendships can ride out trespasses and sins—the greater the hurt or failure, the greater the need for forgiveness, and the greater the value of it when granted. Such relationships truly model God's love for us.

- *Love you when you're unlovable.* We all have moments when we are less than our best. You may say things you really didn't mean or speak in a tone of voice you really didn't want to use. In a good relationship, both parties are very slow to react and are gentle in their responses. A good relationship is marked by mutual patience.

- *Accept you as you are.* I'm not saying that change is impossible or unnecessary. But if you are in a relationship in which you regard the other person as your fix-it project, or you sense that he or she is always trying to change you, that is not a healthy relationship for either party. I'm referring here especially to personality traits and personal habits. If you go into a relationship thinking, *I can get that person to change his personality or quit his terrible habits,* you are likely to be disappointed.

- *Confront you when you are wrong.* You need people who will love you enough to give you helpful insights and strong advice—even when it might be difficult for you to hear . . . those that can lead to improvement in the way you deal with people or approach a problem. You need relationships with people who will challenge you to improve your attitude and your communication skills—in most cases, that means your listening skills. "But," you may say, "isn't that trying to change me?" No. Such a relationship is aimed at bettering who you are, not altering who God made you to be.
- *Serve you.* I am *not* referring to any form of slavery or servitude. I'm referring to maintaining relationships with people who want to help you, who see your need—perhaps before you see it—and move immediately, without any prompting, to assist or rescue you.

Do your relationships bear these characteristics? Is there at least one person in your life who has these qualities?

Of course, you need to be the same kind of person that you are seeking in a relationship. Make it your goal, not only to have a spouse, friend, or associate who fits this profile, but also to be that kind of spouse, friend, or associate to others.

RELATIONSHIPS TO AVOID

Just as there are helpful, highly enjoyable relationships, there are ones you should avoid at all times and at any cost. Do your utmost to avoid entering into any relationship with a person who does the following:

- *Dims your vision.* Such a person questions everything you seek to be or do for God.

- *Discourages you from pursuing your God-given potential.* This person is likely to be jealous of your abilities and your time. They will want you to follow *his or her* agenda, not God's agenda for your life.
- *Drags you down emotionally.* Such a person is always pessimistic, always defeatist, always looking for the reasons why you should not succeed.
- *Derails you from doing things that you know you should do.* He or she tempts you to do evil, not good.
- *Defeats you at every turn,* usually by choosing to be in competition with you in a way that both discourages and frustrates you.
- *Destroys your testimony for Jesus.* This person seeks to destroy your career, your ministry, or who you are in Christ.

OPTIONS IF YOU ARE IN
A NEGATIVE RELATIONSHIP

What should you do if you find yourself in relationship with a person who dims your vision, discourages you, drags you down emotionally, or seeks to derail, defeat, or destroy you? There are really only four things you *can* do:

1. *You can pray for the person or persons to change.* Sometimes they do. Sometimes they don't. Why don't they change? They don't want to. They may choose to be in rebellion before God and, therefore, will always stand in opposition to you.

   Even if the other person doesn't change, your prayer for him is likely to change *you.* You may have greater compassion for him, see the situation more clearly, or gain the wisdom and courage to take whatever action may be necessary.

2. You can give up your dreams and any thought of pursuing your God-given potential. It isn't the course of action I recommend, but it is an option.

3. *You can sever the relationship.* There are times when you need to walk away from a relationship temporarily in order to bring clarity or to work for change. There are also times when you need to end a relationship for your safety, health, or integrity. Sometimes severing a relationship is a matter of saying, "This is not godly, and it is not right. We need to redefine our relationship and enter into a renewed one that is godly and is right." Ending one phase of an ongoing relationship is sometimes very beneficial—it allows you to establish and enter a new phase. The person remains; the relationship changes.

4. You can decide to persevere in pursuing your relationship with God and the potential He has for your life, no matter what others say or do. Set your heart and mind to keep your vision for your life clear and bright. You can find ways to encourage yourself, stay positive, build up yourself, stay on track, sidestep the land mines that are in the path of your relationship, and defeat the devil who is at work behind the scenes. It's not easy, but it's doable.

Let me assure you, it is far better and, in many ways, far easier to evaluate and alter a relationship in its early days than it is to invest years and years in one and then try to change it. Choose your friends and your associates with great prayer and care at that start. Date a person long enough and go through enough experiences to know if the relationship has the right characteristics before you even think about marriage. Test relationships enough to know if the potential of a good, helpful, godly relationship is there for you to pursue.

EVALUATING A POTENTIAL RELATIONSHIP

One challenge we face, of course, is that most people are on their best behavior at the beginning of a relationship. We all want to present ourselves in the best possible light when we enter into a relationship with someone. You need to give yourself sufficient time to get to know a person before you decide whether or not he or she truly will keep your confidence, love you through good times and bad, and be the helpful friend you want to have in your life.

I especially encourage you to do two things:

First, ask the other person about his goals, his dreams, and his perception of the God-given purpose for his life. Ask him what he wants to accomplish or what he hopes to achieve. Listen closely to the goals he expresses that are related to expanding the gospel and the use of his ministry-related gifts. Find out if he even knows his gifts and talents. Ideally, ask these kinds of questions before you reveal fully what you believe God has willed, planned, and purposed for you.

I've heard people say, "Well, I just want to fall in love, get married, and have children." My first thought is, *Then what*? It doesn't take long to fall in love, recite wedding vows, and give birth to children. What happens after the children are grown? What are you willing to support in terms of goals and aspirations in the person you are thinking of marrying? This is true for men as well as women. Will you need to sacrifice anything that you believe God is calling you to do in order for the other person to do what they believe the Lord wants him or her to do? Does God authorize and honor the compromise? Is there anything you'd like to change about the responses a person gives regarding the future he or she envisions?

Second, make certain that both of you are submitted to the Lord Jesus Christ, have accepted Him as Savior, and are seeking to follow the daily leading of God in order to pursue His highest and best. Look for examples of how and when the other person was obedient to God in the past. Watch for evidence of God's work in his life. How loving, kind, patient, joyful, merciful, faithful, generous, and in self-control do you find him to be? Look for these qualities in the way he treats you, his other friends, and close associates. Listen closely to the way he talks about family members, friends, coworkers, and long-time acquaintances.

As you get to know someone, keep in mind these questions:

- Does this person have a godly character? Does his character match up with the qualities described in God's Word as those of a genuine believer in Christ Jesus?
- Is there consistency between what she says she believes and how she acts?
- Is this person truly committed to helping you do your best?
- Does he love you for who you are, or is he seeking a relationship with you because of money, position, or some other superficial reason?
- Can you point to examples in which she is looking out for your best interests?
- Does he have a concept of personal wholeness, and does he desire that for himself as well as for you?
- When the person expresses an opinion, is it wise counsel to you? Does the advice line up with God's Word?
- Is she honest with you—even when she knows her honesty may sting a little? Is she willing to risk rejection in order to confront you in ways that are helpful and constructive?
- Does he accept your personality as well as all your strengths and flaws as a person?
- Is she willing to communicate with you in a way that is transparent and vulnerable?
- Does the person encourage you to pursue your goals and to give your best effort to everything you do?

- Does she stick with you during difficult or trying times?
- Does he enjoy giving to you and receiving what you give him?
- Can you laugh with her? Is your relationship marked by joy, energy, and enthusiasm for life?
- Does the person want for you what God wants for you?

The answers you discover to these questions will tell you a lot that you need to know about this person.

Finally, I encourage you to pray with and for any person that you are seeking to have as a spouse, friend, or close associate. If you can't pray for and with him, consider that a huge red flag. Listen closely to how and what he prays—for himself, for you, and for others.

You can find out a tremendous amount about a person by praying with her. There's much to be learned about her relationship with the Lord and her level of commitment to living the Christian life.

Every good relationship begins in Jesus Christ. You may have acquaintances who are not Christians, but to truly be helpful, your friends must be of like mind and heart about Jesus as Savior and Lord. He is the foundation on which good relationships are built and the core of all good communication. He is the true Source of all mutual giving and receiving, of all genuine love—the kind that lasts and grows over time.

VALUE THE FRIENDS GOD GIVES YOU

Recognize that a faithful and loving spouse, a good friend, or a loyal associate is a valuable gift of God. Thank Him for your friends and loved ones. Pray daily for the people with whom you have a close relationship.

I cannot begin to tell you how blessed I feel to know that people—some of them close, some of them far away—pray for me daily. I also am blessed beyond words to have a core group of close friends with whom I can share virtually any detail of my life. I frankly cannot imagine my life without these friends. I know they are gifts of God to me, and I believe that He has allowed us to have a relationship to further His purposes for me as well as His purposes for each one of them.

The Lord weaves our lives and interconnects us so that as couples, as groups of people, and as the body of Christ, we are mighty testimonies about the love of God and the power He has to transform lives. Every relationship in some way will contribute to God's transformative work in you and through you. Expect that to happen. Your relationships will change you, and if you are in the right kinds of relationships that God honors, your relationships will change you so that you become more like Jesus Christ and become a more effective witness to His saving grace.

To a great extent, your relationships determine the ways in which you pursue your potential and accomplish God's plan your life. Choose to establish relationships that our heavenly Father honors, blesses, and uses for His purposes.

Ask God to help you with choosing and developing your relationships. Pray for Him to send the right people to you. Ask the Lord to help you discern whether a relationship is right for you. Trust God to be an active participant for good in every relationship He encourages you to develop.

A LIFE OF POTENTIAL PURSUED

BILL

Bill was the custodian at a high school for more than 40 years. His boss was the vice principal at the school, but Bill rarely saw him. Over the course of his career, Bill worked for more than a dozen vice principals. He rarely saw his supervisor because Bill knew his job better than his boss knew his job. And Bill believed in his heart that Christ was his ultimate Boss. Bill was self-motivating and kept the school spotless. He didn't require someone telling him what he should do or had to do on any given day.

As Bill put it, Christ was his "Big Boss." So he viewed his work as a mission field. "Those kids are hurting, and I'm supposed to be about helping" was Bill's line. He made a point to befriend the young men and women who were "loners"—the ones often sitting alone in the library or the cafeteria. Bill sought them out in casual, unobtrusive ways to give them a bit of encouragement. His words were never overbearing or inappropriate, but affirming and supportive. From time to time he'd ask simple questions: "Are you getting the hang of geometry?" or "Is history your favorite subject here at school?"

Depending upon the student's answer, Bill had a variety of follow-up answers to suggest that a student might want to go by the counseling office, scout out the tutoring services offered free to all students, or take an aptitude test to discover her real talents. He always left a student with a smile and words along this line: "You'll make it. I know a smart young person when I see one. I'm going to pray that God will help you."

On rare occasions, Bill had an opportunity to say a quick prayer with a student, but it was never anything much beyond, "God, help my young friend. You see the need and You've got the solution." He was always very cautious about the words he spoke to a student, or the prayers he offered. Bill never violated a student's privacy or entered into religious debate.

The vast majority of students never heard a word from Bill. But they did hear him whistling while he worked. Everyone saw the care that he gave to his job, the quality of his work, and the flash of his bright smile.

Several years after Bill retired from his job—at age 80, by the way—students who came back for a class reunion were given a questionnaire. They were asked to identify the person who had affected their lives the most during their high school years. You guessed it—the greatest influencer was Bill. That result was repeated in questionnaires for a number of years. When the school finally set aside a special event to honor Bill, they hung a plaque in the entrance lobby to always remember him.

Students and officials of that school did not know until after Bill died that he had given anonymous college scholarships to more than a thousand students during his career. He left the bulk of his estate to a foundation that purchased computers and gave scholarships to young people overseas who desired to study the Bible using the Internet.

Bill left a letter with his attorney that was published after he died. Part of it read, "I'm not doing this to be anybody special. I'm doing this because that's why God gave me the health and strength to be a good janitor, a good school in which to work, and opportunities to talk to students who needed to hear a positive word."

Did Bill, a school janitor, fulfill his potential? Absolutely!

He did what God had created him to do, to the best of his ability, for as long as possible, as the Lord provided and gave him opportunity.

Oh, by the way, Bill walked with braces on his legs from the age of seventeen.

Did Bill pursue his God-given potential?

No doubt about it!

CHAPTER 9

ESSENTIAL #6:
A BALANCED SCHEDULE

Do you feel stressed out by the schedule you are keeping?

Do you have a good balance of work and play in your life?

Do you find that you are exhausted most of the time?

Or do you experience days that are peaceful, productive, and meaningful?

As you begin to pursue your God-given potential, one of the greatest and most important challenges you face is the way you order your time. A balanced schedule will help you be the person God wants you to be and do the things He wants you to do.

Your time is your life.

Time is irreversible.

It is irreplaceable.

Each of us faces the challenge of using our time wisely.

TIME IS A GIFT FROM GOD

The Bible tells us that time is a gift from God. Our days are in His hands. The psalmist spoke of God's "measuring" our days and giving every person a specific allotment of them. He said, "The LORD knows the days of the upright" (Ps. 37:18). We learn from Ecclesiastes that we have "a time to be born, and a time to die" (3:2).

In various places in the Bible, we read how God set a particular time and season for those He called. From one perspective, we might be quick to conclude that God governs our time completely and leaves nothing to chance—nothing for us to determine. From a broader look at Scripture, however, I believe we are wise to understand that while our days are numbered by the Lord, He gives us tremendous freedom regarding how we choose to live each one. But you and I are responsible for living productively and in a manner that honors and glorifies Him.

Quality of life is a major issue in our world today, especially as the baby boomers in the United States are beginning to hit retirement age. We need to understand that genuine quality of life starts with faith in Jesus Christ. He said, "I have come that they may have life . . . more abundantly" (John 10:10). So God is the One who imparts peace, joy, love, faith, and all of the other characteristics to the human heart that contribute to our overall health and well-being. Furthermore, quality of life is not determined by how much money someone has or what career she has. It is marked by satisfaction and fulfillment in work and relationships that have purpose, meaning, and opportunities to serve and grow.

The stingy, greedy, sinful, lustful, wasteful person who is totally self-centered and self-gratifying does *not* experience quality of life at any age, much less old age. By comparison, a person who is joyful, generous, loving, kind, faithful, and peaceful can, and often does, enjoy a tremendously high-quality life—even without many material possessions, comforts, or luxuries.

Unrepentant sinners know no peace and, therefore, can have no genuine quality of life. Those who have received the free gifts of salvation and forgiveness made possible through accepting Jesus Christ as Lord and Savior have true, lasting peace. As a result, they experience the highest possible quality of life here on earth.

So it all begins inside us and affects our external choices and decisions. A major factor related to our quality of life is time management. How we choose to spend the hours of our days, the days of our weeks, and the weeks of our years is vital. Over time, we develop habits and routines that frame and reflect our lifestyle.

To make the most of your life and your God-given opportunities, you must value the time that He has ordained for you and seek to fill it with those things that are of highest value.

The apostle Paul wrote to the Ephesians about time: "See then that you walk circumspectly, not as fools but as wise, redeeming the time, because the days are evil" (Eph. 5:15–16). In saying that the days are evil, Paul was noting the cultural and spiritual decay all around him in the Roman Empire. The bent of the entire world seemed to be toward wickedness. Certainly, we can draw a similar conclusion about our world today.

I identify two key phrases in this passage. First, Paul called Christians to "walk circumspectly, not as fools but as wise." Believers are to make the most of every opportunity. You and I are to seek God's wisdom about what we should do and the priorities we should set each hour, day, week, month, and so forth. We should have goals and plans for the time given to us. To walk circumspectly is to weigh risks and consequences before taking action. God wants us to evaluate our opportunities and take full advantage of ones through which we can share the gospel and produce spiritual fruit.

The second key phrase is "redeeming the time." Christians are to value every minute. We are not to waste time or consider it unimportant. Every minute counts.

To make the most of every opportunity and value our time appropriately, we must actively manage and bring order to our schedules so we can live balanced, productive, and meaningful lives.

SECONDS AND MINUTES COUNT

Many people seem to have little regard for the seconds and minutes of their lives. I sometimes hear people ask one another, "What are you doing?" and the answer often is, "Nothing much," or "Oh, I'm not doing anything." What sad statements! When I hear those kinds of responses, something in me rises up and shouts, *Why is that the case?* You will not live these seconds and minutes again. You will not have another opportunity to live today. There is no repeat or replay button for the hour that just passed. Seconds tick away into minutes, minutes tick away into hours, hours tick away into days, days tick away into weeks, weeks tick away into months, months tick away into years, and years tick away until a lifetime is over.

This idea is not just important for those who see more sand in the bottom half of the hour glass than in the top half. Never think, *I've got plenty of time left.* Never say, "Oh, I'm only 24 or 38 or 46 or 50" or any other age. You do not know how much time you have left to accomplish God's will, plan and purpose for you. None of us know the length of our days—only the Father knows that. You may be far closer to the end of your life than you think.

I do not say that to scare you or to make you feel helpless or hopeless. I simply want to awaken you and motivate you to make the most of the time you have today, tomorrow, and the rest of your life.

You are to pursue your potential right now.

THE STEWARDSHIP OF YOUR TIME

When you reach the age of 70, you will have lived 840 months. That's 25,550 days or 613,200 hours or 36,792,000 minutes—give or take a few minutes and hours associated with leap years. Every bit of that time is holy because it is a gift from a holy God. It is to be valued and spent in ways that honor the Giver.

You are called to be a steward of your time. God has given you time to live out His will, plan, and purpose. To waste time is to be a poor steward. It is to fail—minute by minute, hour by hour—to accomplish all that God has called and equipped you to do from the moment of your creation.

Let me challenge your thinking in two main areas of time management.

1. Think of Time as an Investment

While we are called to live day by day, you and I are also called to fill our days with things that will bring maximum reward in the future. What we do today sets the foundation for the life we can and will live tomorrow.

I have seen this among my friends who invested their money wisely over the years. They gave a portion of every dollar they earned toward ministry to spread the gospel and build up the body of Christ. They also saved a portion of their earnings for the future life they hoped to have. The remainder of their money was invested in a quality life. While possessions are not over valued, each is treated with respect so that they lasted and gave the greatest amount of service possible.

Through the years, many people I know have invested in their physical health. They have adopted healthy habits—exercising, managing their diet, and taking the supplements their bodies require. They have made an effort to give themselves the greatest possibility of living with minimal pain and degeneration, and a maximum amount of energy, strength, and flexibility, long into their eighties and nineties—and perhaps beyond.

Now there are no guarantees that if you invest your time and money wisely, or do all the right things you know to do for good health, you will avoid all financial or physical problems. Only God determines our ultimate "success" here on earth. Accidents happen. Diseases strike. Financial markets collapse beyond our personal control. But let's also own up to the truth that a large majority of people who have sufficient funds in their so-called retirement years planned and invested toward the income level they hoped to have in their later years. Financially sound retirement doesn't happen by accident or automatically. We can't wake up one day and say, "I think I'll retire," and then ask, "Where's the money to do that?" In all likelihood, the funds won't be there unless we have made provision for sound investment long before that moment.

In like manner, there is a great deal that we can do to maximize our health in the future. The truth is, most of the dreaded diseases of our time—cancer, heart disease, diabetes, and other degenerative autoimmune diseases—are greatly impacted by our lifestyle choices. We can choose what we eat, drink, inhale, or otherwise take substances into our bodies. We control the amount of sleep we routinely get, how much we exercise, how often we relax, the quality of the air we breathe, the amount of stress we internalize, and the way we think and use our faith.

I'm not going to tell you how to live or which habits you should give up and which new ones you should adopt. But I do appeal strongly to you: live today in the way that will give you the greatest quality of life in the years ahead. How you use your time now is a very serious predictor of how you could be spending your hours and days in the future.

Let me also call your attention to this truth: there is a reason for you to have the maximum amount of health and financial security down the road. But it has nothing to do with your desire to engage in your favorite hobby every day or sit by a pool and watch the world go by. It has everything to do with the need for you to have the energy and resources to fulfill all that God is calling and preparing you to do.

Whatever your life's purpose and work, you need energy, strength, and material resources to get the job done with quality, productivity, and impact. God wants you to map out your time and resources today so you can fill your future with purposeful, meaningful activity and ministry. Ultimately, you are to fill your days with activities and conversations that have the potential for eternal reward.

2. Approach Your Schedule in Terms of Balance

A schedule is a set of time segments, and a task is assigned for each one. You can, and should, do many tasks in any given day. Each takes time. The key is to prioritize your tasks and then allot the appropriate time to complete them. The ultimate challenge is to have your priorities in the right order and balance your schedule.

Consider the life of Christ. Jesus certainly lived a balanced life.

THE BALANCED LIFE OF JESUS

You may think that Jesus lived nonstop teaching, preaching, and performing miracles—everything from roadside encounters with people in need to feeding thousands of people on a grassy hillside. There was more to His life than that. Jesus had a public ministry, but He also had private times with His closest friends and associates. And the Son of God had intensely personal times when He was alone with His heavenly Father.

Prayer

We read in Mark 1:35 that Jesus was up before dawn every morning to pray. Prayer includes making requests of God and offering thanksgiving and praise. The apostle Paul made the point that "by prayer and supplication, with thanksgiving," we should make our requests known to the Lord (Phil. 4:6). Psalm 100 says this about the proper prelude to prayer:

> *Enter into His gates with thanksgiving,*
> *And into His courts with praise.*
> *Be thankful to Him, and bless His name. (v. 4)*

Most of prayer should be spent listening to God and finding out what the Lord desires for you to do in your immediate and long-term future. Prayer is a time to talk things over with God, just as you would share your most intimate concerns, fears, worries, and questions with your closest friend or confidante. Much of prayer should be spent telling the Lord about the things that give you joy. Too many people resort to prayer only when they are in a crisis, or they make their daily prayers a litany of problems, needs, and troubles. Prayer is a time for rejoicing with the Lord over the victories that He has won in and through your life.

Jesus taught His disciples to "seek first the kingdom of God and His righteousness" and everything else necessary would be added to their lives (Matt. 6:33). He said that if His disciples lived with that perspective, they would have no need to worry. Jesus made prayer His top priority—it was first on His schedule each day. First priority became first action.

Time with Family and Friends

We do not know many details about Jesus' time with family. But we do know that the Lord was with His mother, Mary, at a family wedding in Cana and that He provided for Mary in His dying moments on the cross. As the eldest son in a Jewish family, Jesus had responsibility for His mother after the death of Joseph. He would have fulfilled that responsibility in every way. Jesus loved His mother and cared for her.

Christ had a number of friends, including Martha, Lazarus, and Mary in Bethany. The Bible tells us that He loved this family, and we know that He visited them on more than one occasion.

Jesus took time for conversations and meals with many people for various reasons. He was a welcome guest in the homes of people such as Zacchaeus. Jesus spent one-on-one time with Nicodemus and mingled with those who were considered to be sinners in the eyes of the religious leaders of His day. We do not know all the people whom Christ counted as friends, but we do know He was friendly, approachable, and sociable.

We also know that Jesus laughed and rejoiced over those who received what He gave to them.

He accepted dinner invitations and celebrated the Jewish feasts with various groups of people. And we have no reason to think that these social events were burdens to Him. Jesus delighted in the goodness of God the Father, and He appreciated the kindness of those who provided for Him and ministered to His daily needs for food, shelter, and other provisions.

On the night before the crucifixion, Jesus said to His closest associates, "I have called you friends" (John 15:15). He prayed that His heavenly Father would make them "one in Us" and that the glory God had given to Him would be given to them (John 17:21–22). Jesus said to them, "Greater love has no one than this, than to lay down one's life for his friends" (John 15:13).

We do not know how many close friends Jesus had, but we do know that He spent what appears to be extra time with Peter, James, and John. He had close fellowship with these three men who were active with Him in ministry.

Work

Of course, Jesus had an active schedule of preaching, teaching, and healing. Those were the three dimensions of Christ's work during the last three years of His life. There is no indication, however, that He conducted His ministry work in a frantic or impersonal way.

The question-and-answer method of teaching was common to Jewish tradition in that day, as well as in many Hebrew schools today. Jesus interacted with those He was teaching. Many times, rabbis taught as they walked with their disciples, using everyday objects, experiences, and aspects of nature as tools. This type of ministry teaching requires extra time. Jesus did not just stroll into a setting, speak for ten minutes, and walk away. He prayed for people who came to Him with their needs and answered those who had sincere questions.

In three short years of active ministry, Jesus walked hundreds of miles, going from place to place—including trips to Jerusalem for feasts. All able-bodied Jewish men were required to go to there at least three times a year to celebrate the feasts of Passover, Pentecost, and Tabernacles. Jesus kept those feasts and used them as opportunities to teach and minister in the temple.

He spoke in synagogues and in large open-air meetings.

He actively engaged in conversations with people, even His enemies.

He spent small group time with His chosen apostles, speaking to them about deeper truths, explaining His parables, and preparing them for the day when He would not be physically present with them.

Without doubt, we have a responsibility for working. You and I have a responsibility for producing something that is of benefit to someone else—a responsibility to serve the world in some way. The word *retirement* is not in the Bible. We are to live every day of our lives with purpose and with an eye toward accomplishing something worthy of presenting to the Lord as an offering of our praise.

God values our efforts. He is the One who takes what we do and turns it into an accomplishment or a success. You may think that you have engineered your success in the past, or that you are capable of engineering it in the future. That is not the case. You are responsible for making the effort and devoting your time and energy to the task you believe God has set before you. The results are His domain. He is the One who turns your action into souls won, lives changed, needs met, and doors opened for the gospel.

The good news in this is that God will take even the smallest sincere effort on your part, multiply it, and use it for your good and the good of others. You can only plant a seed—you cannot grow it. You can only do what you know you should do—you cannot ensure your health, prosperity, or security.

God calls us to act. And He responds with His infinite power, presence, and wisdom to turn our actions into accomplishments.

Let me be very direct in saying to you:

Being active does not automatically mean that you are effective.

Being busy does not automatically mean that you are productive.

Being overbooked and overextended does not automatically mean that you are profitable.

At one point in my life, I devoted much of my non-Bible reading to the biographies of great men who had profound, far-reaching ministries and impact on the world. I did not realize it then, but most of those biographies focused almost entirely on what a person did, how much he accomplished, and how effective he was in his work. There was little mention of his downtime—his recreational activities or getaways with friends. There was little information about what made him smile, much less what made him laugh. There was little investigation of the stress he might have been feeling as he went about his work.

Being a workaholic is as damaging as being slothful. Both are bad stewardship of time and energy.

It's entirely acceptable to be inactive for a season. It's another thing to be lazy or slothful. God expects you to live your life with purpose in all things. A lazy, slothful person has no purpose for the time she wastes by goofing off, procrastinating, or engaging in pleasurable activities that have no real meaning or benefit. Separating yourself from the world for a while to rest is purposeful. It takes only a short period of time to become rejuvenated. An entire lifetime of self-imposed rest is a waste.

Worship Time

Someone once asked me, "Did Jesus go to church?" Yes, He did. Throughout the Gospels, we find instances where Jesus was present in the synagogue of a city on the Sabbath. He joined with others in hearing God's Word read from the scrolls, and sometimes He was handed a Torah to read aloud from it. He joined in the praise and prayers that were a regular part of Jewish worship. Jesus knew the Scriptures very well—He recited them as part of His ministry, He spoke or sang the songs we know as the Psalms, and He referred to both the Law and the Prophets in His speaking. Jesus learned the Scriptures, prayers, and Psalms as part of a godly Jewish family. Spending time in the synagogue was as natural and normal for Him as being in His own home.

As Jesus became more famous during the last year or two of His life, crowds of people clamored for Him and gathered around Him virtually everywhere He went. Jesus likely stopped at small synagogues less frequently and spoke more often to very large groups in the temple, where there was room for hundreds of people to gather.

Anytime someone says, "I don't have time to go to church," his schedule is out of balance.

Some people have said to me, "I don't get anything out of church." My response is, "Then you are probably going to the wrong church!"

Others say, "I spend personal quality time with the Lord. I don't need other people around me." The truth is, very few people who say that actually spend personal quality time with the Lord. You do need to be in worship with other people. You need the ministry gifts that they can give to you, and you need to give them the gifts that God has placed into your life. The church is intended to be a place of giving and receiving—each person sharing with others around him all of the encouragement, admonition, instruction, support, insight, help, and joy that he is capable of giving.

Being around other Christians is an opportunity to grow, be strengthened, and better equipped to face the challenges of daily life. If you are not hearing preaching that convicts you, admonishes you, instructs you, and encourages you, you need to find a church where you will hear that kind of preaching.

I once asked a woman where she attended church. I knew she lived in a sparsely populated area of our nation, so she likely had to drive a significant distance to get to a church. She replied, "I attend Bedside Baptist." I didn't understand her joke at first, and I asked with innocent sincerity,

"Who is the pastor there?" Later, I realized that my reply was probably the most profound one I could have given.

By the way, that woman tried to justify her answer by saying, "When I wake up on Sunday morning, I just turn on my television set and watch *In Touch*." I said, "Well, that's good but not good enough." You need to be involved in a church so you can hear what others are saying about God and tell others what you know about Him—from your reading and study of His Word and from your service to others His name.

If you reach conclusions about God and your faith solely on your own, you are going to be in grave danger of developing errant theology. You risk holding on to a belief system that is not balanced by the practical application of living out the Christian life in relationship with other people.

There is something wonderfully healthy about singing and praising God within a fellowship of like-minded believers. You are refreshed as you surround yourself with others who love the Lord.

The Bible tells us, "Let us consider one another in order to stir up love and good works, not forsaking the assembling of ourselves together, as is the manner of some, but exhorting one another, and so much the more as you see the Day approaching" (Heb. 10:24–25).

A Time to Read, Study, or Discuss God's Word

Many people do not realize that the Jewish men of Jesus' day had a custom of reading, studying, and discussing the Scriptures every night after dinner. It was not a once-in-a-while activity but a regular six-days-a-week activity. While the women were cleaning up the supper dishes and putting the children to bed, the men of a neighborhood gathered to talk about Scripture. Usually it was a passage the rabbis through the years had designated for study that particular day.

The Jewish day began at sunset. Righteous Jews kept this custom of immersing themselves in the Scriptures so that all through the night, the truth of God could be folded into their subconscious by the Holy Spirit. They went to sleep each night with their minds filled with God's Word.

It was also a good time to enjoy the comfort gained from connecting with their neighbors. They relaxed and focused on the eternal truth of God, rather than on the problems of the day just lived.

This custom was mostly for the men, but some women gathered to sit and listen to what was being discussed. Mary, the sister of Martha and Lazarus, was apparently one woman who highly valued an opportunity to listen to conversation about God's Word (Luke 10:38–42).

Most people structure their evening hours so differently today. It is too common to stare at a television set and watch hour after hour of programs laced with violence, fantasy adventure, sexual innuendo, commercials, and all the rest.

Can you see the wisdom in turning off the TV? Spend one evening devoting yourself to God's Word and with friends who want to talk about the principles, precepts, and glory of the Lord, and I guarantee that you will not miss your programs one bit.

It is very likely that Jesus encountered Nicodemus during such an evening of Scripture study and discussion. Read the third chapter of John's gospel and be grateful for what was discussed that night.

Relaxation and Rest

Jesus also relaxed and rested. In Mark 6, we read how the apostles came to Christ to give a full report of what they had heard and done after being sent out to minister. Jesus said to them, "Come aside by yourselves to a deserted place and rest a while." The Bible tells us, "There were many coming and going, and they did not even have time to eat. So they departed to a deserted place in the boat by themselves" (vv. 30–32). When times became too stressful, or when He and His associates were exhausted, Jesus was wise enough to withdraw for rest and relaxation.

The more intensely you engage in your work and ministry, the more you need time apart from the pressures of life. It will restore your energy, rejuvenate your soul, refresh your relationship with family and friends, and renew your walk with the Lord. This goes beyond daily prayer. It is extended time to sleep, engage in calming and quiet activities, and take into your life beauty and silence.

In the early years of my ministry, I felt that if I wasn't preaching, preparing to preach, or following up with a new believer just after I had preached that I must be sinning against God. I did not live a balanced life. As a result, my physical health and the overall well-being of my mind and emotions suffered. When I was a young man, I was physically sick far more days a year than I am now. Looking back, I know that much of my sickness was directly related to stress and to my work-work-work-and-only-work schedule.

I allowed my vocation to be a pressure-cooker. There was always something I felt I should be reading, studying, researching, preparing, planning, or doing. It wasn't just the number of activities I was engaged in during any given week—it was the pressure I placed on myself to do them all as perfectly as I could and without any help. While I still try to always look my best, be my best, and do my best, I do not feel pressure to be perfect. I no longer think that I am the only one capable of doing a job or that I am supposed to do every job.

Ironically, today I am preaching to far more people than in those early years. I believe I am teaching better and with greater impact on individual lives than ever, and I lead a much more balanced life. I still can become weary from work, but my work does not create pressure in me. It is not stressful to me. I can walk away from work for times of relaxation and not feel one ounce of guilt. That's a very healthy place to be.

I know many people who go on vacation and come home needing another vacation to recover. They think that just getting away from their routine and daily responsibilities will give them rest. That rarely happens. You need to be very intentional about what you choose to do and not do if you truly want to relax and be refreshed.

Through the years, I have gone to a place on a number of occasions where I can walk the beaches for hours, stop to pray when I want to pray, pause to watch the waves, explore the tidal pools when I want to do that, soak up the sun, and breathe in the fresh sea air.

Mountain places also hold special appeal for me. There's something about being out on a mountain trail far from a city, seeing the canopy of stars overhead at night, being surrounded by forests, confronted with unexpected vistas, the surprise of rushing streams, and beautiful flower-filled meadows. Few things are more wonderful or more refreshing to me.

On other occasions, the most restful and relaxing thing I can do is go to the darkroom in my home to print photographs. Or these days, I go to my "light room." It allows me to clearly see and print photographs that I have taken with a digital camera.

In whatever way I personally choose to rest and relax, I find myself refreshed by a lack of noise and of man-made visual stimuli—no billboards, rush-hour traffic, or bustling crowds. There is rest in setting aside unstructured time. I find it very beneficial to schedule time that can be filled with spontaneous activity. That may seem like a contradiction, but it is not. Set aside an hour or two a week for alone time, and when that time comes, determine what you will do that brings relaxation.

I know a young man who set aside two hours a week while he was in college to go night fishing with a friend. They often went to a river that flowed by an electric company, so they always had light. Wearing their waders, they walked into the river and often caught large fish that they would quickly release. To some, this may seem to be wasted time that could have been better spent in study. But this young man found that he had sufficient energy to study only when he took this time to fish.

Jesus had fun. He was no doubt an enjoyable person to be around. How do I know that? Because children loved to be with Him and around Him. And children do not enjoy being with adults who are serious, angry, bitter, or hostile. They respond to people who are loving and gentle, and who know how to laugh and have fun.

Children no doubt saw Jesus as a man who was quick to hug them and invite them to come close, who told them stories they could understand and enjoy, who listened to their tales, and who liked to laugh with them. Jesus said He came to show us the Father. And if you think that God is only a serious, angry, bitter, hostile, highly judgmental figure sitting on a throne up yonder waiting to pounce on your every misdeed, well, you haven't really read your Bible or looked closely at the life of Christ.

See Jesus surrounded by children. Watch Him with spiritual eyes as He interacts with them. Observe how He listens to, cares for, holds, and has fun with them. That's the way your heavenly Father wants to interact with you. He delights in you and cherishes time with you. God loves watching your amazement at what He does on your behalf. I am convinced that He desires for His people to have the most fun of anybody on earth.

Choose your fun wisely. Engage in activities that do not abuse your body or pollute your mind and heart. Thousands of activities can bring a spring to your step and a smile to your soul.

Sleep

Jesus had no trouble sleeping. He was even able to sleep soundly in the middle of a tremendous storm that was threatening to capsize the fishing boat He was sailing in with His disciples (Matt. 8:23–26). Jesus trusted His heavenly Father with His waking hours and sleeping hours.

I recently read a survey indicating that most adults in our society are sleep deprived. Deprivation is not a term to take lightly. This survey was not concerned with people getting up fifteen minutes or a half hour earlier than normal. The subjects stated that they routinely got only four to five hours of sleep per night—which was only about 50 to 60 percent of what is required for a normal healthy adult to completely rejuvenate the body's cells and tissues.

Sleep is not an option. It is not a nicety of life, but a necessity. During deep, sound sleep, the mind processes all the bits of information gleaned from the day and sorts it in appropriate ways for recall and use. During deep, sound sleep, many of the body's hormone levels are rebalanced and reset for the next day's activities. During deep, sound sleep, dead cells are replaced with new ones. During deep, sound sleep, T cells (cells linked to immunity) multiply fastest and act in the most effective ways to bring healing to areas of the body that have been damaged in accidents or by viruses and bacterial infection. That is why sleep is one of the most therapeutically beneficial prescriptions for those struggling with physical ailments, mental disorders, or emotional exhaustion.

God made you to be alert and vibrant during your waking hours. He also made you to require sleep. It benefits your body and your mind.

Review your schedule. Do you need to get more sleep?

Do not deny or diminish what you perceive to be a need for sleep. Those who do not get enough of it report far more accidents, sickness, trouble in relationships, problems at work, frustration, anxiety, worry, and depression. Sleep-deprived people tend to have fewer satisfactory relationships and receive fewer promotions. They fall more and fail more. They are less productive, do poorer quality work, and are less efficient than those who get enough sleep. They use more medicines and take more prescriptions.

Studies also show that children and teenagers tend to be sleep deprived due to late hours watching television, playing video games, or surfing the Internet. Young people who don't get enough sleep are more anxious about life, earn lower grades, have more conflicts with peers, and express more anger, hostility, and resentment toward adults who are authority figures. Sleep-deprived students do more poorly in athletic events, and they tend to rely more on sugary foods—including soft drinks and junk food—to give them energy. This, in turn, creates a blood-sugar problem that may be one of the main causes for diabetes among young people and for ongoing nutritional imbalances. Blood-sugar swings have been linked to behavioral problems that are parallel to sleep deprivation.

What are we to conclude? Most people need more sleep!

Adjusting your schedule to allow for more sleep may be one of the most important decisions you make when it comes to pursuing your God-given potential.

Fitness and Health

At all times, Jesus lived a healthy life.

He did not work out three times a week in a gym or exercise on home fitness equipment. The plain and simple fact is that He didn't need to! That was not because He was fully God and fully man. It's because He routinely engaged in one of the most beneficial exercises any able-bodied person can do—walking.

Apart from riding a donkey into the city of Jerusalem on what we now call Palm Sunday, Jesus does not appear to have ridden on any animal or in any cart during His active ministry. Only rarely did He take a boat across the Sea of Galilee rather than walk around it. Much of the terrain He traveled was hill and mountain country. Most of the roads in Jesus' time were not paved, so His walking was not easy walking. Jesus got plenty of exercise, likely on a daily basis.

When it came to foods, Jesus ate according to the Jewish laws of His day. His diet was filled with vegetables, fruits, fish, whole grains, olives, olive oil, and, very likely, a form of yogurt-like cheese made from goat's milk. Only rarely did He eat red meat, and He abstained completely from those foods and beverages that were described in the Law of Moses as being unclean. Today, people call this the Mediterranean diet, and it is one of the healthiest ways to eat.

Some people say, "God doesn't care how much or what I eat. He doesn't restrict me in any of these areas. He doesn't care whether I exercise or not." The truth is, God does care what you put into your body and how you take care of it. He created your body and allows you to occupy it. The apostle Paul emphasized the point: "Do you not know that your body is the temple of the Holy Spirit who is in you, whom you have from God, and you are not your own?" (1 Cor. 6:19). God expects you to take care of your "temple" and to treat your body with respect.

The Bible is very clear: you do not have the right to do whatever you want to do with your body. God commands you to abstain from anything that has the potential to bring you harm or cause death. That includes substances that you might take out of a desire to escape or to feel good. That will only drive you deeper into despair and ultimately make you feel bad, not only in your body but also in your soul. God does not want you addicted to anything. He is jealous for your devotion.

His Word also commands us to "flee sexual immorality" (1 Cor. 6:18). The Father's plan for you is to keep you from relationships that can tear at your heart, rip apart your family, or tarnish your testimony for Christ. He wants to keep you from all manner of disease and degradation that accompany a promiscuous lifestyle.

Did Jesus live a healthy, pure lifestyle? Absolutely. Does He call you to live that kind of life? Yes. Will He help you make the changes you need to make? No doubt about it.

Living a pure and healthy life is a choice you must make. If you have a sedentary life or you work at a desk all day, you may need to add specific times of exercise to your schedule. It will help you develop a strong heart and cardiovascular system, strong muscles, and flexible joints. If you have been living on fast food, you may need to schedule more time to shop for groceries and to prepare nutritious meals.

There is no doubt that exercise and nutrition are vital to good health and part of God's plan and purpose for you. Your responsibility is to eat right, get enough exercise, get enough sleep, drink enough pure water, and breathe as much fresh, clean air as possible.

Just as you are to be a good steward of your time and possessions,

God calls you to be a good steward of your body. Taking good care of your health requires time.

A SCHEDULE ADAPTED
FOR YOUR GOD-GIVEN PURPOSE

A balanced schedule is structured according to the purpose that God has established for your life.

Jesus did only what He knew with certainty the Father authorized Him to do. I have no doubt that the Son talked with His heavenly Father about his schedule every morning. I can almost hear Jesus asking, "Should I go here? Should I go there? Should I contact this person or that person? How should I structure my afternoon? What plans should I put into motion for future days this week or this month?"

Do you talk to God that way about your schedule? Or do you hurl yourself into an almost frantic routine each day? Do you rush from place to place and chore to chore, thinking that in all of your busyness you are accomplishing real work or establishing real relationships?

Jesus controlled His schedule according to the Father's plan. His schedule did not rule Him.

Furthermore, Christ approached His schedule in three ways that are particularly relevant to us today:

1. Jesus never attempted to justify His schedule or make excuses for any aspect of it. He didn't say, as many people do today, "I just had to get away," or "Please forgive me, but I just don't have time to . . ." Jesus lived His life without relying on the approval of other people. He sought only to please His heavenly Father and to do what God told Him to do.
2. Jesus never was hurried or flustered when it came to His schedule. He did not rush from place to place. In fact, for purposes

that were a mystery to His close followers, He willfully waited in Jericho even after He received news that Lazarus was very ill. We know in retrospect that He did that for the wonderful purpose of raising Lazarus from the dead. But at the time, Jesus' disciples certainly did not understand His apparent laid-back approach to the situation.

3. Jesus did not find His schedule to be stressful. He did the things that were important and let the unimportant things go by.

THREE QUESTIONS AND
THREE CATEGORIES OF ACTIVITY

The Lord has dealt with me about my schedule in recent months, so I evaluated how I was spending my time—daily, weekly, and monthly. I began by asking myself, *What am I doing?* I suspect that few people ever stop to consider that question. I made a list of all the things I did during most days, or in a given week or month, and the results were a bit staggering to me. I put down even the smallest activity or chore. Dozens of items filled the list.

Second, I asked, *Which of these things is absolutely vital to my fulfilling my potential and doing what God has created me to be and do?* I circled those items.

I took a short break before I returned to my list. Then I asked the Lord to show me if any of the things I had circled were my idea. I wanted confirmation that those things I perceived to be part of His will, plan, and purpose truly were His will, plan, and purpose for me.

Then I asked a third question: *What do I really need to do, what do I need to let others do, and what doesn't need to be done at all?* I wrote those headings at the top of a piece of paper and began to put the overall list of things I was doing into those three categories. I invite you to do a similar exercise as you take control of your schedule:

Things I Must Do   *Things I Should Delegate*   *Things I Should Ignore*

I discovered a number of things that simply did not need to be done. I had a longer list of things that could be delegated. And there were things that I personally and actively needed to do—not just occasionally, but consistently.

I came away from that exercise with my eyes wide open. I also had a new determination that I was going to make some changes! And I did.

Under the heading "Things I Must Do," I put those things I had circled from my long "doing" list. I encourage you in this—the things that God has purposed for you need to be at the top of your "must do" list for any day, week, month, or even year. Certainly some relatively small things related to personal hygiene as well as some very good things that strengthen family relationships and friendships are important to include in this list. But at the very top of the list should be the things that God speaks to your heart, *I made you to do* this!

Then I began to delegate and eliminate. Various things that could be given to other people were handed off. Various things that did not need to be done—by me, by others on my behalf, or by others for the sake of others—were eliminated.

Many people are faced with a time-or-money opportunity. You may be wiser to hire another person to do some things on your behalf. If your time is better spent doing something that will produce more income than what it would cost to have someone else do a particular chore, then you are wise to hire someone and devote yourself to what is productive and profitable. At times, of course, you may not have the money to hire someone to do that chore. In those instances, you need to make a plan for earning more, saving more, or streamlining a chore. This is a second valuable exercise you can undertake in taking responsibility for your schedule. If there are things that you think you should delegate but cannot, make a plan for moving from your current situation to the situation that you desire and that you know is God's desire for you.

I encourage you also to identify the things in your life that you are doing because you previously had to do them, but now you no longer must do them. Many people take on a responsibility or chore that should have been temporary, and it becomes such a habit that they continue in it long after they could have and should have let it go.

I already know that I should, and will, revisit my three-category list in the near future. This exercise is not something that is done just once. Life brings new opportunities and situations every day.

Every vineyard and orchard owner knows that vines and trees need to be pruned every year. The dead wood must be eliminated. The live wood needs to be pruned for greater growth. The same is true for your schedule. There's dead wood—activities that are unnecessary or unfruitful that need to be cut out. There are things that perhaps should be combined or restructured for greater productivity and impact.

EVALUATE THE PRIORITIES
AND BALANCE OF YOUR SCHEDULE

We know that Jesus spent time every day in these activities:

- Prayer
- Time with family and friends

- Work, which in Jesus' case was the work of full-time ministry
- Scripture reading, study, and discussion

He spent time every week in worship.

He spent time in rest and relaxation.

What about your schedule? How have you chosen to fill your time and with what activities?

Also ask these questions about your schedule:

- What stresses me?
- What makes me feel hurried, anxious, or rushed?
- What am I doing as a result of others insisting that I act or behave in a certain way? Is their insistence justified against what God has called and purposed for me to do?

Some answers to these questions may be difficult. You may need to make tough choices about your work or your relationships.

A while back, I found that I was much more productive, less stressed, and more relaxed in my dealings with people if I did not drive myself to some of my appointments. I mean that literally. Driving the freeways of my city is stressful. Having a driver allows me to make phone calls, collect my thoughts on my way to a speaking opportunity, or review my list of things to do. It helps me arrive at my destination focused, relaxed, and ready to jump immediately into the tasks awaiting me.

This is just one change that the Lord led me to make. It may not be an example that is relevant or possible in your life. But there no doubt are some changes you can make that will minimize stress, streamline your day, and help you get more out of every hour you are awake or at work. Ask God to reveal those changes to you. Once you are aware of them, act on them! Pray frequently and regularly for the Lord to help you remain flexible and to be wise in the ways you simplify your daily life.

HOW MUCH TIME SHOULD BE ALLOTTED?

Not only do you need to ask the Lord how He wants you to set priorities for various activities; you need to ask Him how much time He wants you to spend doing them.

People often say, "It's not how much time you spend; it's the quality of the time you spend." While that is true to a great degree, it is not true in all cases. A child spells love *T-I-M-E*. Your son or daughter wants you far more than he or she wants material things. Children value the *presence* of a parent more than presents. He may not require huge amounts of your time, but he does want to know that you are available to him and that you value the time spent with him. Your child wants to know that he can be with you when he needs you or that she can talk with you when she needs to talk.

The same is very likely true for your spouse. It can be true for people you work with or your closest friends. Your spouse, immediate family members, friends, and associates need to know that they have access to you, and that you value time with them.

It takes time to know that another person loves you or to show someone that you love him or her. Any relationship marked by love requires an investment of quality time and availability.

Any truly meaningful conversation takes time. You can try to deal in sound bites as you go through life's routine, but if that's all you exchange with a spouse, close associate, or friend, your relationship will never grow very deep. Talk things over with someone close to you. Give your insights. Gain his insights. Aim your conversation at meaningful and challenging topics, especially ones that are mutually helpful in your understanding of the Lord, the Christian life, and your motivations and beliefs.

Through the years, I have often found that as I am talking with a friend, I gain new insights into what I personally believe, think, and feel. I may have been totally oblivious to some of my inner motivations or responses—but in a conversation that is open, transparent, and loving, I discover more about myself and the way the human heart and mind work. In the process, I discover more about how God works and the ongoing, intimate relationship and conversations He desires to have with each one of us.

REEVALUATE YOUR SCHEDULE PERIODICALLY

I tend to look at my schedule annually and then again monthly, weekly, and daily. Before I go to bed at night, I use a three-by-five-inch index card to make a brief list of what I intend to do the next day. I go to bed with an awareness of what I believe I am facing the next day. It is amazing to me how often I write a problem on my card and wake up in the morning with the solution. God seems to work in my mind and subconscious during the night so that the creative answer comes even before I have time to tackle the problem. Even if that answer does not come to me overnight, I awaken with direction for my day. I submit that to the Lord in prayer to confirm if I am on the right track. And then I'm ready to go!

The main challenge for me in developing my schedule is to keep it from becoming fragmented. A fragmented schedule commits too little time to complete any one activity or task in a high-quality way. Five minutes of practice a day is not enough to develop a major skill. Two minutes of Bible reading a day—one minute in the morning and one at night—is not enough. A person can build so many different things into a schedule, and give so little time to each activity, that they become dissatisfied and frustrated. There's no sense of real peace, satisfaction, or accomplishment when too much is attempted in too little time.

Feelings of frustration and anxiety can also arise if you allow temporary distractions and crises to keep you from doing the things that are on your must-do list. People who travel a lot in their work frequently encounter this problem. The plane and train schedules do not fit their normal routine. They are out of balance when they are on the road and stay that way for a day or two after returning home. It takes tremendous discipline to avoid schedule fragmentation and disruption.

Once you have balanced your schedule, you must be disciplined and diligent in order to keep it that way.

MAINTAINING A BALANCED SCHEDULE

How do you maintain a balanced schedule once you have developed it? Perhaps the greatest asset is having someone in your life to whom you are accountable for your time.

Ultimately, you are accountable to God for the use of your time. But I refer here to your having someone in your life who keeps track of and confronts you about your schedule. Note that I did not use the word *combats* you, nor did I use the phrase "is confrontational." The person you accept to be your accountability partner in this area should be someone you trust and respect, and someone who loves you. He should have no fear in confronting you about your time management. His words to you should be clear and direct. He should know you well enough to sense if you are being accurate in your appraisal of your behavior. In other words, he should be able to know that you are telling the whole truth about your schedule. For this kind of accountability to work, you need to set an appointment periodically so you are forced to confront your schedule in an unavoidable, undeniable way.

I have that kind of accountability partner. I have talked with this man in such detailed and highly transparent ways for so many years that, at times, I suspect he may know me better than I know myself. I have given him the right and privilege to ask me about any aspect of my life and to confront me anytime he thinks I need a reality check about my schedule. He has full permission to reprimand me anytime he thinks I am moving into error. I have said to him, "If you ever see me headed in the wrong direction, you need to say to me, 'I don't think that is the wise thing to do.' Then I will listen to you and heed your counsel."

It takes a long time to develop a trust relationship with a Christian friend who will keep confidential what you share with him and be candid with you from a sound, biblical viewpoint. But let me assure you, nothing is more valuable in helping you stay on track toward reaching your full potential.

Invite the Lord to hold you accountable for your schedule. He'll do it. The Holy Spirit is the ultimate time manager and accountability partner.

A LIFE OF POTENTIAL PURSUED

TRINA

Trina felt absolutely overwhelmed by her life. The mother of two-year-old twins and a four-year-old, she was on the go constantly. She worked part-time in her husband's franchise business, mostly by helping him with marketing plans and bookkeeping. Her parents were in poor health and looked to Trina to help them with transportation and some basic housekeeping and personal-care chores. Her friends from college days didn't understand why she couldn't break away to watch movies with them or go out to lunch.

She told a friend, "I'm on the go from six in the morning to midnight. Most days, the only thing I do for myself is run a brush through my hair and take a quick shower."

To complicate matters, Trina's husband was spending very long hours at work and was rarely available to help her with the children, home chores, or yard care. Everywhere she looked, she saw something that needed to be picked up, washed, fixed, or weeded.

Finally, Trina talked things over with her aunt: "I'm getting to the point where I'm too tired to give my husband the love and attention he needs, too tired to play with my children and help them and teach them as only a mother can, and too tired to even care very much that I'm failing in virtually every area that is important to me as a wife, mother, daughter, and woman."

Trina's aunt was a wise, godly woman who knew how to manage time and to organize space. In fact, she founded and owned a business that designed closet space and helped people organize their clothing and possessions. Trina's aunt said, "I'm coming over on Saturday, and we're going to look at what you might be able to do to get your head above water."

Over the next three months, Trina dramatically changed her schedule. She and her husband talked things over and decided that it was financially wiser to hire a bookkeeper at the business and to consult with a professional ad agency about marketing plans for the future. Trina streamlined some chores around the house and built time into her schedule for both personal relaxation and morning fellowship with the Lord.

"That was the biggest change," she later told her friend. "My aunt made me realize that my entire schedule needed to be submitted to God for His review. I realized right away that I wasn't starting my day out right. I set my alarm for a half hour earlier than usual, which meant that I needed to get to bed a half hour earlier, which meant that the children needed to be in their beds earlier, and so it went. The time I started spending with the Lord each morning—in prayer and Bible reading—was just what I needed for greater peace of mind and clarity about what was really important in my life."

As part of her personal relaxation time, Trina pursued her favorite hobby, making scrapbooks. A couple of years went by and when the older child entered school, she arranged for the two younger children to be in a Christian play-and-learn center two days a week. With her kids occupied elsewhere, Trina started a business creating professional scrapbooks for companies, organizations, and several wealthy clients who traveled a great deal. She loved the interaction with other people, and on countless occasions, she found opportunities to talk to people about the Lord.

"It was an easy thing to do," she said. "Some of my clients who traveled had wonderful photos of cathedrals they had visited in various countries, and that was always an open door for talking about God."

Trina also had this insight: "I realized that those frantic days with my young children were a season in my life. My children didn't care if everything was starched and sparkling. They wanted time with Mom. I gave them what they needed most, and I took that perspective into every area of my life. I try to give others what they need most, which is not necessarily what I think they need or what I need. It freed me tremendously."

Is Trina pursuing her God-given potential?

I believe she is!

CHAPTER 10

ESSENTIAL #7:
TAKING
GOD-APPROVED RISKS

D o you like to play it safe?

Do you insist on guarantees?

Are you afraid of change?

Do you like to explore new possibilities?

If you truly are going to pursue your God-given potential, you are going to find yourself in situations and face opportunities that will require decisions and action. Some of those decisions and actions may appear risky to you.

Does God want you to live a life that is totally risk free? No.

Your potential is the sum of all the possibilities that God has for your life. And the truth is that you have absolutely no way to comprehend all of the possibilities that an all-wise, all-knowing, infinite God sees. You cannot know with your finite mind and your limited perspective all that He knows.

A significant amount of risk is involved in trusting God in all things, in all relationships, in all choices, and in all decisions. Risk is part of the very nature of faith:

- putting our belief in God whom we cannot see but still experience,
- putting our faith in His promise to work all things to our benefit, even if we cannot understand what must occur to get us from where we are to where we hope to be,
- putting our faith in the love of God to transform us in ways that we cannot even begin to imagine or expect.

Let me remind you of one of the greatest risk-takers of all time. Jesus had just multiplied five loaves and two fish to feed five thousand people. The day had drawn to a close, and this is what happened:

Jesus made His disciples get into the boat and go before Him to the other side, while He sent the multitudes away. And when He had sent the multitudes away, He went up on a mountain by Himself to pray. Now when evening came, He was alone there. But the boat was now in the middle of the sea, tossed by the waves, for the wind was contrary.

Now in the fourth watch of the night Jesus went to them, walking on the sea. And when the disciples saw Him walking on the sea, they were troubled, saying, "It is a ghost!" And they cried out for fear.

But immediately Jesus spoke to them, saying, "Be of good cheer! It is I; do not be afraid."

And Peter answered Him and said, "Lord, if it is You, command me to come to You on the water."

So He said, "Come." And when Peter had come down out of the boat, he walked on the water to go to Jesus. But when he saw that the wind was boisterous, he was afraid; and beginning to sink he cried out, saying, "Lord, save me!"

And immediately Jesus stretched out His hand and caught him, and said to him, "O you of little faith, why did you doubt?" And when they got into the boat, the wind ceased.

Then those who were in the boat came and worshiped Him, saying, "Truly You are the Son of God." (Matt. 14:22–33)

People sometimes criticize Peter for putting his eyes on the wind, doubting that he could do what he was already doing, and sinking. Yet besides Jesus, Peter was the only person in the Bible who walked on water!

The disciple was willing to leave the boat, step out on water, and begin to walk toward Jesus. Would you have been willing to take that risk?

Stop to consider for a moment what happened in Peter as a result of that experience. Do you think he was encouraged or discouraged in his faith? Do you think he said to himself, *Well, that'll teach me never to get out of a boat and try to walk on the waves of a stormy sea*? Or do you think he said, *I just walked on water! Jesus said I could and I did. If I had just continued to keep my eyes on Him and off the wind-swept waves, I might still be walking on water. It's possible for a man to walk on water. Whatever Jesus tells me to do, I can do it! Whatever Jesus calls me to do, I can accomplish it. I just need to keep my eyes on Him.*

I believe that experience deepened Peter's faith and made him willing to take great risks later in his life and ministry—long after Jesus ascended into heaven.

Here's why I believe that. Just two chapters later in the gospel of Matthew is the account of Jesus and His disciples at a place called Caesarea Philippi. The palace of Philip, one of King Herod's sons, was located there. In Philip's attempts to appease Rome and give honor to Caesar, he allowed a number of shrines to be constructed to pagan gods. Idols or images of many of these gods had been set in niches which were carved into the stone at the base of the mountain that rose to the north of Caesarea Philippi.

In Matthew 16, we read:

[Jesus] asked His disciples, saying, "Who do men say that I, the Son of Man, am?"

So they said, "Some say John the Baptist, some Elijah, and others Jeremiah or one of the prophets."

He said to them, "But who do you say that I am?"

Simon Peter answered and said, "You are the Christ, the Son of the living God."

Jesus answered and said to him, "Blessed are you, Simon Bar-Jonah, for flesh and blood has not revealed this to you, but My Father who is in heaven. And I also say to you that you are Peter, and on this rock I will build My church, and the gates of Hades shall not prevail against it. And I will give you the keys of the kingdom of heaven, and whatever you bind on earth will be bound in heaven, and whatever you loose on earth will be loosed in heaven." (vv. 13–19)

Jesus recognized Peter's potential to be a tremendous leader. His name Simon literally referred to a kind of reed that grows along the edges of the Sea of Galilee. They are so pliable as they wave in the breeze and sway in the water that they are of no use on dry land. Peter gave Jesus an answer that was strong in faith, and Jesus acknowledged his faith and said, "You are Peter." That new name for Simon refers to a rock. Something solid. Something that can be trusted as a foundation. Jesus further stated that Peter's declaration of faith was the very rock on which He would build the church. And indeed, through the ages, the resounding message of the church has been that Jesus is the Christ, the Son of the living God. This is the declaration of His supremacy over all other gods. He is the Cornerstone of our faith.

Peter, the only apostle to walk on water, had heard Jesus chide him for having "little faith." He did not take offense at the Lord's' words—he knew Jesus was telling him the truth. After sinking in a storm-tossed sea, Peter appeared to have determined in himself that he was going to become a person of greater faith. Just a short while later, Peter was the only apostle to declare that Jesus is the Christ, the Son of God. He was the first of the twelve to make that statement about the Lord. Peter's faith in Jesus was then rock solid!

What you see as a risk from your perspective could be the very situation that God wants to use to strengthen your faith. What you think holds the potential for loss or danger, God may very well be using to strengthen your character. What you view as taking a chance, very possibly could be what God will use to carry you one giant step closer to reaching your full potential.

VARYING PERCEPTIONS OF RISK

People perceive risk differently.

Some people enjoy living on the edge. I consider mountain climbers among those people. I have seen climbers scale the vertical, sheer face of Half Dome in Yosemite National Park, and I get fearful just watching them. As far as I am concerned, what they are doing is borderline ridiculous. And it is certainly not something that I desire to do. However, to mountain climbers, that adventure is exhilarating, fantastic, and challenging. Nothing could be more exciting. The thrill of reaching the top is worth the risk that their equipment might fail or that they might lose their grip and fall.

When I watch NASCAR drivers, I feel a bit scared on their behalf too. Traveling just inches from other vehicles around an oval track at 200 or more miles-per-hour seems like an unnecessary risk to me. But the drivers readily say that they never feel more confident or enthusiastic about life than when they are pushing their cars and themselves to the limit.

They know that a crash or an engine failure could occur any moment, but that doesn't stop them from competing.

Other people are so miserable in their current condition that they are willing to take risks in hopes of effecting a change. Years ago, refugees frequently left Cuba in little boats, facing the threat of sharks, stormy seas, and faulty navigation equipment in an attempt to reach the U.S. mainland and a life of freedom and opportunity. For them, the risk was worth taking because life as they knew it was so limiting.

Still others take risks because they are in pursuit of a cause they consider to be noble and worthy. U.S. servicemen and servicewomen put themselves in harm's way for the cause of freedom. Many missionaries through the years have taken risks for the cause of the gospel.

The perception of risk is highly personal.

THE NATURE OF A RISK

Consider the nature of a risk. It involves the possibility of suffering danger or a loss of some kind. We often associate taking risks with doing something that holds out the possibility of rejection or failure. There are elements of fear and disappointment that are part of every risk we take. The flip side of a risk is the possibility that we just might experience a great blessing or reward!

How do we determine which opportunities to pursue in our quest to reach our full potential? We are not to make decisions based on the degree of perceived risk. Rather, we are to make decisions solely on the basis of what God says.

The truth is, choosing to do something solely on the basis of your limited understanding and ability leaves too much to chance. But pursuing God's command—an action or decision that is the product of His unlimited wisdom and power—is not risky at all. If it is God's idea, we cannot fail in our pursuit of it.

The challenge we face as opportunities come our way is to understand what God is doing and where He is leading.

THE CHARACTERISTICS
OF GOD'S CHALLENGES

God has many ways to confirm that the challenge before us is from Him. You and I can know with certainty that we have heard from Him. How?

First, God always gives us opportunities that challenge who we are already and that are designed to move us to a new level of what we are already doing. Consider Peter again. He was accustomed to taking on challenges. He was a bold, courageous, take-charge guy. He might come across in the Scriptures as a bit bold or brash at times, but Peter also had a good heart. The day he met Jesus, Peter provided a boat from which the Lord could preach. When He was finished, Jesus told Peter to let down his nets. Reluctantly, the future apostle agreed and soon was overwhelmed by the magnitude of his catch. Peter was so humbled by the miracle of fish that he fell at Jesus' feet and cried, "Depart from me, for I am a sinful man, O Lord!" (Luke 5:8). He did not feel worthy or adequate of the Savior's love, care, and provision.

The apostles were frightened to see Jesus walking on the water. But the Lord spoke to that fear and said, "Be of good cheer! It is I; do not be afraid." Peter, being the man of action that he was, did not say, "Well, Jesus, if that's You, get in the boat with us and calm this storm." No, Peter took a look at Jesus and said to himself, *Jesus is a man like I'm a man. He's more than a man, but He has a physical body like I do. If He can walk on water, perhaps I can too!* Peter saw a challenge, and he said, "Lord, if it is You, command me to come to You on the water." Jesus responded to that and said, "Come!" (Matt. 14:27–29).

In that instance, Peter had strong confidence that if Jesus said he could do something, then he would do it! That's the point of the confidence and faith that the Lord desires for us to have.

The challenges that He presents to us are always consistent with our God-given gifts and talents, as well as our personalities. The Lord does not call us to do something that is totally opposite of who He made us to be. Nor would God present a challenge that requires more than the abilities and propensities that He already has placed in us. Any test or opportunity from the Lord will be in keeping with who we are so that we might become more than we are. The challenge will be related to what we are already doing so that we might be elevated to something even greater.

Second, God always calls us to *something.* Our heavenly Father does not call us to quit something so that we might then do nothing for the rest of our days. For example, God called Abram to leave Haran, the place where he had traveled with his father, Terah, away from Ur, which was the land of Abram's youth. Abram had lived in Haran for many years. It had become his home. Suddenly the Lord spoke to him and said, "Get out of your country, from your family and from your father's house." But God didn't just call Abram to leave; He called him specifically to go "to a land that I will show you." God did not give all the details, but He made sure that Abram knew with confidence that a new land and a new future awaited him.

God also assured Abram that in this new place his descendants were going to be a great nation, he would be personally blessed, and his name would be great. God said,

> *You shall be a blessing.*
> *I will bless those who bless you,*
> *And I will curse him who curses you;*
> *And in you all the families of the earth shall be blessed.* (Gen. 12:1–3)

Talk about a challenge! Think about getting up from where you are, leaving everything behind, and going to a new place filled with new opportunities far beyond anything you have ever dreamed.

At that point, Abram did not have any heirs. Yet God said he would be a great nation. Abram had people who worked with him and for him, but he did not have a son. To be a great nation meant that Abram was still going to have children. He was seventy years old at the time, so that was a serious miracle promise.

If God leads you to stop something, He is preparing for you to do something else. He is about to transition you from where you are to the even better, more rewarding, more fulfilling, and more purposeful future.

God is always leading you toward:

- something greater,
- something better,
- something more meaningful,
- something more joyful, and
- something more fulfilling.

Furthermore, God said that in the new place Abram's name would be great and that he would be a blessing so that he could bless others. That brings me to my next point.

Third, God sets before us a challenge that holds the opportunity for blessings beyond ourselves. A challenge from the Lord is not only for your good but also for the advancement, healing, and fulfillment of His plan in the lives of others. If an opportunity is only for you or your immediate family, it very likely is not from God.

Stop to consider that Moses was already "free" of Pharaoh's court and the Egyptian way of life when the Lord called him to return to Egypt. Moses was certainly a reluctant leader of the Israelites and a very reluctant speaker. The challenge God gave him was for the advancement of all Moses' people, far beyond his immediate family or the families of his siblings, Aaron and Miriam.

Moses faced a risk in returning to the court of Pharaoh. Why? Because Moses had fled from Pharaoh's court after killing an Egyptian in defense of a Jewish slave. He was a murderer on the run. Moses knew that Pharaoh could have ordered his execution at any time during his series of demands that resulted in horrible plagues.

Nothing about Moses' return to Pharaoh's court held out the potential for great personal blessing and reward, but the potential for great blessing and reward was present for Moses' people. In the end, Moses certainly received personal blessing and reward. He was able to live among his people, experience amazing encounters with almighty God, have the satisfaction of leading his people to freedom, and watch them develop into a nation. Self-gratification and self-advancement were not part of Moses' agenda.

The same was true for Gideon. When God called him, Gideon was secretly threshing wheat in a winepress. He feared that his actions might be discovered by Midianites who had invaded Israel. The Lord's angelic messenger greeted Gideon with the words, "The LORD is with you, you mighty man of valor!" (Judg. 6:12). Gideon neither saw that God was with him—after all, his people were being greatly oppressed—nor felt like a man of valor. The Lord saw potential that Gideon did not see.

As Gideon obeyed God's challenges, he took risks. In fact, with each experience the risk level seemed to increase. The Midianite army had tens of thousands of soldiers. Gideon knew that he was actually facing three armies—drawn from the Midianites, the Amalekites, and the people of the East. The Bible tells us that those soldiers were "lying in the valley as numerous as locusts; and their camels were without number, as the sand by the seashore in multitude" (Judg. 7:12).

Gideon managed to amass an army of 32,000 to fight for Israel. But God said, "That's too many." So 22,000 went home. Only 10,000 remained. But the Lord said, "That's still too many." Finally Gideon was down to 300 men, and they went into battle. Each man carried a trumpet in one hand, a knapsack of provisions slung over his shoulder, and a clay pitcher with a torch that could be lit inside it. God used the most unlikely means to gain a powerful victory over the Midianites (Judg. 6–8).

Was the series of battles Gideon fought solely for his benefit? Not at all. Gideon was certainly blessed. He rose to leadership and had sons and grandsons whom the people wanted to carry on his leadership. He lived to experience 40 years of freedom and peace after Midian had been subdued (Judg. 8:28). But Gideon's obedience in pursuing God's potential was not solely or primarily for his benefit. All of the children of Israel were blessed.

Esther, too, was willing to risk her life to speak on behalf of her nation. An evil man named Haman was intent upon killing all of the Jews in Persia. Esther, as the chosen queen, knew that if she went into her husband's presence without his having sent for her, she could be put to death. The challenge held out before her was filled with risk. Esther said to her relative Mordecai, who had told her about Haman's intentions, "Gather all the Jews who are present in Shushan, and fast for me; neither eat nor drink for three days, night or day. My maids and I will fast likewise. And so I will go to the king, which is against the law; and if I perish, I perish!" (Est. 4:16).

The king received Esther, and two banquets later, it was Haman who was facing death, not the Jews. The benefit for Esther was not only that her life was spared. She also was given a tremendous opportunity to bring blessing upon her people. Their lives were spared, and a festival of perpetual remembrance—a day of rest, feasting, and gladness—was established so that the Jews would continue to live and be honored by the generations to come.

Did Abram, Moses, Gideon, and Esther have moments of fear and doubt? I am certain each of them did because they all were human beings. In fact, I believe every person who is challenged to a new task or level of responsibility is going to have moments of doubt, fear, hesitation, and second-guessing. Those emotions seem to accompany all great challenges. The examples of people such as Peter, Abram, Moses, Gideon, and Esther are evidence that fear and doubt can and must be overcome by faith.

If you act on what you believe is a challenge from God and suddenly are gripped with fear or doubt, you need to:

- put your eyes back on Jesus. Stop looking at the negative circumstances. Stop listening to the naysayer who doesn't think you are capable or worthy of anything good from God.
- cry out to the Father and ask Him to confirm His presence, power, and love.

I am confident that every person who cries out to God is not only heard by Him, but also helped by Him.

Fourth, God will confirm His presence as you pursue the challenge He has set before you.

People have asked me, "How far did Peter walk on the water?" My answer: "Far enough!" It might have been a few feet or a few yards. Even two steps walking on water is more than any other person has ever walked as far as I know. Peter walked far enough to know that he could do great things if he trusted Jesus fully and followed the Lord's command. Furthermore, we read that Peter walked back to the boat with Jesus.

Take heart in the fact that Jesus did not condemn Peter for doubting or withdraw opportunity from him because he was afraid. The Lord lifted up His disciple as he sank, chided him for his lack of faith, and then enabled him a second time to walk on the waves back to the boat.

Jesus did not abandon Peter or allow him to drown. He remained with Peter and walked with him. And as far as we know, Jesus never again brought up the fact that Peter stumbled over a whitecap in the Sea of Galilee.

As a believer, the Lord is with you. He remains with you. He does not forsake you nor does He abandon you, even if you have fear, doubt, or hesitation.

Fifth, God's challenges to you are always accompanied by the enabling power of the Holy Spirit. The Lord does not call you without equipping you with His divine presence. Jesus said that the Holy Spirit would give us both comfort and counsel as we seek to implement God's plans for our lives.

The Holy Spirit will nudge you in your spirit, "Do this. Don't go there. Say this. Avoid that person." He will remind you of the words and deeds of Jesus. He will remind you of God's commandments and Bible stories of mighty victories. He will remind you of the sure and lasting promises of God's Word.

In the most exciting ways, the Holy Spirit will give you His creative and productive ideas.

Years ago when our church was still located very close to downtown Atlanta, I had a sense that we were becoming boxed in. The sanctuary was capable of seating more than 2,000 people, but the parking lot had only a couple of hundred parking spaces. The math didn't work.

When I recognized this discrepancy, took a look around, and realized the church was surrounded by buildings and businesses of various types, the sanctuary was not full every Sunday. And sometimes, the parking lot wasn't full. But I knew that God was at work in our midst. The sanctuary would be full one day—for multiple Sunday morning services—and the parking lot problem was going to be serious.

I learned one day that a particular piece of ground close to the church was going on the market. The Holy Spirit spoke in my heart as boldly as I have ever heard Him, *Buy it.* I spoke to our board about it. The board was reluctant but eventually agreed that the risk of the investment was worth taking.

Another piece of property became available. So I took that issue to the Lord. And in no uncertain terms, He spoke to my heart, *Buy it.* Again, the board was hesitant but agreed.

Bit by bit, piece of property by piece of property, we acquired sufficient land to expand our campus and to provide parking for churchgoers. The day arrived when the church was filled to overflowing, and the parking was still insufficient.

Someone asked me, "Where would you move if you left downtown?" I pointed to a specific area on the map of greater Atlanta, a piece of property along a major freeway of the city. I was quickly assured that no property was available there. I sensed in my spirit, however, that we were moving, and it would be to that area.

What happened? Two things occurred almost simultaneously. A suitable piece of property became available in the area I had envisioned a new church, right on the freeway. And we were offered a price for the total property we had acquired in downtown Atlanta—which had increased dramatically in value from the time of our purchase. We were able to make the move and expand not only our ministry, but also our international outreach in a matter of months.

Did all this happen without moments of fear, hesitation, and doubt? Let me assure you that any challenge from God is accompanied by those moments, even when it comes to what appear to be very solid business deals. There's always a concern about whether buyers will actually buy and sellers will actually sell. There was some concern that people who had been attending the church in the downtown area would not want to drive "up north" to the new location. In reality, some left, but even more came. Our church has almost doubled its membership from the "downtown years."

Someone might say, "Well, you just used good business sense." Let me assure you, that's not what happened. The Holy Spirit prompted me in ways that I knew it was Him, and He knew that I knew it was Him. Furthermore, His timing was perfect. We bought low and sold high. We sold at precisely the right time. Sellers and buyers came together at exactly the right moment. We built for flexibility and expansion. Again and again, we faced a challenge, but each time it came with the fullness of God's presence, provision, and wisdom.

WHY DON'T PEOPLE RESPOND TO GOD'S CHALLENGES?

Why don't all people respond quickly and enthusiastically to all of God's challenges? I believe there are several major reasons.

First, we want to stay in control. And we don't want to experience change that we do not initiate and do not control.

God's challenges always require a degree of submission and trust. When the Lord presents a new opportunity, you can expect to:

- go somewhere you've never been,
- do something you've never done,
- give something you've never given,
- surrender something you've never surrendered before,
- love someone you've never thought was lovable,
- forgive someone you've never forgiven,
- become something you've never been, and
- trust God for something you've never trusted Him for.

If you truly want all that the Father has for you, then you are going to have to face your pride, yield your life to God, and give up any demand for control.

Second, we are afraid. Sometimes we fear that God will fail us or we will be hurt. Are you afraid of how the Lord may change your life? His Word tells you that God will remove only what is bad for you, and He will ask of you only what will lead to what is best for you.

Based on everything I know about God and His Word, I assure you that He will always do the right thing. He always knows the right way. He always leads you to success. His will is always accomplished—if not now, later; if not through you, through someone who is willing to obey Him and step up to His challenges.

The opposite of faith is fear. There are some things that we should fear. I think it is very healthy, for example, to fear a rattlesnake or a grizzly bear. I am not at all interested in putting God to any test regarding either one of those creatures.

Other fears bind us, sometimes to the point of paralyzing us. We don't speak because we fear what others might think of us or that they might reject us. We don't act because we are afraid that we will not live up to expectations or that we will be a disappointment. We don't pursue our potential because we worry that our dreams may not be *possible* to achieve and we will be ridiculed for thinking they are. In many cases, we do not step out in faith because we have these fears about God or our faith:

- We fear that we haven't heard Him correctly.
- We fear that we expect something too wonderful or too great— and in some way we are not worthy of such an awesome thing in our lives. This is sometimes true when it comes to pursuing a relationship or a goal that we want to set. We aren't sure in the deepest recesses of our hearts that God will choose to give us what we desire.
- We fear that others will not understand our commitment to the Lord or our confidence that He is leading and guiding us.

These fears are at the core of risk. We must overcome them with faith when we are reluctant to respond to God's challenges.

Speak to your fear, doubt, and hesitation. Remind yourself:

- God desires only the best for me.
- He is in control of all things.
- The Lord can do what I cannot possibly do to ensure that I will succeed.
- My heavenly Father loves me unconditionally and has promised never to abandon me, forsake me, or fail me.
- God wants me to receive all the rewards and blessings He has planned and prepared for me.

Make a list of Bible verses that speak to you in a special way about His promises, provision, protection, and love for you. Memorize those passages. Recite them to yourself often.

Third, we listen to the devil's lies rather than God's truth.

Part of the reluctance in actively pursuing the Lord's will, plan, and purpose is spiritual opposition. The last thing Satan wants is for you to be and do all that God has created you to be and do. Face up to that.

Resist the enemy's lies associated with your potential. Ignore what he whispers about your inadequacy. Tell the devil the truth:

- "I can't, but God can."
- "I'm not in charge. God is! The Lord has assured me in His Word that He is in me, will always be with me, and will live out His life through me."
- "I'm not responsible for the level of success. God is."
- "I didn't make the plan for my life. God did."
- "I didn't build into my life any of the gifts I have or the opportunities God is giving me. This is His doing."

As a friend of mine says, "When the devil comes around to say, 'You shouldn't try that,' I tell him, 'Take your suggestion to Upper Management. The office of my CEO is the throne room of heaven. I was told to do this, authorized to do this, and have joy about doing this. Therefore, I'm forging ahead whether you like it or not. So, get out of my way, Devil, and stay silent, or the angels who have been dispatched to help me will run right over you or knock you at least halfway back to hell.'"

The Bible assures us that when we resist the lies of the devil, he must flee from us (James 4:7). When we stand up to him, he must back down.

These main reasons—control, fear, and spiritual opposition—are what we can resolve when we live by faith. The Bible tells us that as Christians,

"We walk by faith, not by sight" (2 Cor. 5:7). God is always taking us into new realms—things that we cannot see clearly, but things that we *believe* are His plan.

SHUT THE DOOR ON REGRET

What happens if you do not act when God sends opportunity, even if risk seems to be involved? You will very likely have regrets down the road. Those who refuse to take the risk of obeying and following God's leading are going to miss the fullness of the reward that He has for them in heaven.

I would much rather try and fail than never try at all. I choose not to live with regret.

If you are unwilling to accept the risk of pursuing your potential, you will never be who God created and intends for you to be. You will never achieve what He has equipped you to achieve, and you will never discover the fullness of His love for you.

Don't rationalize your disobedience.

Don't justify your failure to respond.

Choose, instead, to welcome every God-given opportunity that He sends your way!

A LIFE OF POTENTIAL PURSUED

SUSAN

Susan grew up in a family that had very little regard for formal education. Her family had always been blue-collar factory workers, and Susan saw no reason to aspire to be anything else. The Monday morning after she graduated from high school, she joined her mother, father, and two older brothers at the factory.

She was highly productive, very efficient, and had a cheerful attitude. Her supervisor quickly recognized all of these traits, and before long, Susan was made a first-line supervisor.

During her annual review, she was asked if she found her job fulfilling. Susan said yes, but she was open to new challenges. The person doing the review wanted to know more about her interests and wondered whether Susan might be willing to train for a different job that paid a higher salary. She was quick to accept that challenge.

For the next few weeks, Susan explored various options within the company. She had never owned or operated a computer before—apart from one class in high school. She was fascinated with the possibility of working with computers. But Susan openly admitted that she should probably take a typing class and a computer class before being qualified for any position in that area of the company.

Fortunately for Susan, her company offered several practical skills–based training programs during evening hours. On her own time, she learned to type using a typewriter and a computer keyboard, which meant she was also learning computer skills along the way.

Susan met again with human resources personnel and discussed areas where she might work with her newly developed skills. The job counselor asked her, "Do you like words more than math or math more than words?" Susan wasn't really drawn to either option. She had never enjoyed math class, and she didn't consider herself to be a very good writer or a very accurate speller. Then the job counselor asked her the questions that changed her life. He said, "Do you like working with people more than machines?" Susan said, "Yes." The job counselor followed up, "Do you like solving problems?" She again replied, "Yes!" Then he asked, "Do you enjoy a good puzzle or a good mystery? Are you eager to find the solution or figure out the answers to a problem?" Susan replied a third time, "Yes!"

The next month, Susan moved into the customer service division, answering phone calls from vendors and tracking down the answers to their questions and concerns. She took all of her energy and good attitude into that position, and within five years, she was named head of the vendor relations department.

Before long, Susan was training and helping others become outstanding customer service problem solvers. A few years later, she was named an associate vice president in the customer service division.

There's no telling how high Susan may go in this company.

What happened in her life?

Susan discovered the core talents and abilities that God had placed in her.

She was willing to develop those talents.

She was willing to learn new things and change her daily work.

She was willing to take on a new challenge.

Susan never lost her ability to work well with other people. Her relationships with people above and below her on the company's organizational chart remained highly positive, as did her relationships with the people she served over the phone and the coworkers with whom she worked daily.

The higher the profile Susan gained at the factory, the more opportunities she had to mentor new hires. A number of these employees were people that Susan befriended as they entered the work world straight from high school. She knew how they felt, including their fears and hopes and, at times, their low feelings of self-worth. She shared with them how God helped her to face her fears and gave her courage to try new things. Over time, some of those people asked Susan about her faith in God.

At last count, she has led thirty-four people to faith in Jesus Christ.

Is Susan pursuing her God-given potential?

Every day!

CHAPTER 11

THE ONGOING
PURSUIT

As you begin to pursue your God-given potential, you will face immediate challenges in your first steps along this journey toward your eternal destiny. You also will face the ongoing, daily challenge of maintaining steadfast growth.

I strongly encourage you to do two things.

First, broaden your input, even as you increasingly focus your output.

Second, accept only the opportunities that you know for certain are God's plan for you.

BROADER INPUT, FOCUSED OUTPUT

The Lord intends for you to keep learning and having new godly experiences all your life. The more you fulfill your potential, the more you will have a need for input, which includes knowledge and wisdom from others and wisdom that comes from experience and application.

I would never encourage you to pursue or receive anything that is contrary to purity or God's commands. But I strongly encourage you to expand your horizons. Be open to new ways to express your gifts or to serve others. Recognize that you can draw insights from many areas of information—even areas that don't seem remotely connected to your career field.

Years ago when I was a young pastor, I accepted an invitation to preach at a revival miles away from my home church. After the services had ended, the pastor handed me a small brown sack and said, "I hope I do not offend you in giving you these books, but I felt impressed that they may be of benefit to you." I thanked him and left, opening the sack only hours later. Inside I found two books, one of which I later realized was a classic in the business field. It was titled *Think and Grow Rich* by Napoleon Hill. I thought that was a rather odd title for a fellow pastor to be giving to me, knowing that my heart was fully in the ministry and that financial wealth had no appeal to me.

As I began to read that little book, however, I could hardly put it down. Page after page held nuggets of information and truth that I could apply directly to building a church, winning the lost, and encouraging growth in those who were already saved. The principles in that book excited me and instructed me simultaneously. I was not interested in building wealth or acquiring material things, but I could see that God desired for me to make adjustments in my thinking, my attitude, and my planning that could make me very rich in spiritual fruit. I began to apply the principles of that book to my endeavors as a pastor, and I discovered they worked! For years, I read *Think and Grow Rich* every year to remind myself that the truth of God is not just for one career field. It is for all manner of work and ministry.

That book by Napoleon Hill opened my eyes to the value of motivational books. These books were not part of my college education or my seminary training. They were not part of the curriculum for my doctoral degree in theology. In retrospect, I am convinced they should have been required reading for my academic studies. I added a large number and wide variety of these books to my personal library because I saw in each a nugget or two (sometimes more) of truth about influencing others to accept Christ, motivating individuals toward greater godliness, and "selling" people on the idea of living the Christian life with joy, faith, hope, and consistency.

I do not at all criticize the category of books that people call self-help. We all need help. Many of them help people shake off the lethargy and apathy that have them stuck in a settled-for life. These books can provide practical advice and inspiration for pursuing one's God-given potential.

The key to gaining benefit from these books is this: always weigh their advice against the Word of God. Always be on the alert about how the principles presented relate to the truth taught by Jesus Christ. Many times you will find that the commandments, statutes, and precepts of Scripture are packaged in new terms or unusual phraseology to catch a person's attention or trigger a person's faith.

For decades, many in the church have backed away from the areas of psychiatry, psychology, and mental or emotional illness. The plain and simple fact, however, is that Christians can become mentally or emotionally ill the same way non-Christians can. The more we understand how the mind and body work, and how they interact with the spirit, the better off the church will be.

Not long ago, I was surprised to learn that a dear friend subscribes to a very scientific academic magazine. Science—especially formal science—seems far from what this person enjoys the most. This woman is very much into the arts—literature, fine art, classical music, and so forth. When I expressed my surprise, she said, "I see all kinds of applications that directly relate to creativity. The way God's universe functions—from the unique flight patterns of birds to the migration patterns of fish—hold spiritual lessons for me. And the intricacy of the Creator's patterns and ideas, at both the microscopic level and the grand scale of the universe, reveals to me more and more about His nature and about the creative capacity He has placed in each person." I had never thought of it that way.

When this friend showed me some of the Hubble Space Telescope's photos of far-off galaxies, I was stunned to see that each system, with its millions of stars, has a unique shape, pattern, and color. Science is just one way of approaching and gaining understanding about the glory of God that fills the universe.

PURSUE ONLY THOSE OPPORTUNITIES SENT BY GOD

There was a period in my life when a number of people seemed to think that I should leave the ministry and go into business. They thought that I should give up my work as the pastor of a church to only write books and speak at motivational seminars. The people who made these suggestions had all sorts of reasons for giving me their opinion. A small portion of what they said made sense—at least enough sense that I went to my knees in prayer about their advice.

I asked the Lord, "Do You want me to do something else? Do You want me to leave the place I have been and enter these areas that are being held out to me?" The answer was a clear "no" to both questions. God made it very obvious that I was to continue doing what He had created, called, and equipped me to do until He told me otherwise.

As you go through life, you will face countless opportunities for new memberships, situations, investments, associations, relationships, career opportunities, alliances, and mergers. Not every opportunity is a good one. And with even greater certainty I can tell you, not all of them are sent by God.

Take every opportunity to the Lord. Ask Him, "Should I explore this? Should I do this? Should I try this? Should I commit to this?"

The opportunity may appear to be within the parameters of your gifts and desires. It may seem to be consistent with God's design for your life and your potential. But you cannot know with certainty that an opportunity is from the Lord *unless you ask Him about it!* Don't assume that you alone can discern the path you should walk. In fact, take the opposite approach. Determine that you cannot discern your path apart from the direct, active guidance and leading of the Holy Spirit.

"But how will I know His answer?" people ask. I've learned that when people ask that question, they rarely have prayed for the Holy Spirit to guide them and confirm what they should do. The first step is to intentionally ask Him these basic questions:

- What?
- Who?
- When?
- Where?
- How?
- With what goal or purpose?

Listen for the Holy Spirit's answers. Don't act until you know that you've heard from Him.

If something is presented to you as "you must decide right now or the opportunity ends," take that as a sign that your answer should be no. An opportunity tied to a rushed or ironclad ultimatum is rarely from God.

If I had listened to what other people said to me about how I should invest my life, I cannot begin to fathom all that I might have missed or lost.

God did not put you on this earth to have people pull you this way and that so you can do things for their benefit, their advancement, and their goals. Certainly, we are to work with one another and help one another the best we can. But no person is to be the "author and finisher" of our lives apart from God. Christ did not redeem you on the cross so you could become another person's slave—employee, yes, but slave, no. He did not redeem you to do the bidding of another person, giving 100 percent of your time and energy to satisfy his or her wants and desires. No. You are to help when and how you can help in godly, affirming ways. But you are to do Christ's bidding and no one else's.

God has a wonderful way of weaving together everyone's personal plans and purposes. When things function according to His will, people are helping one another even as they are working with or for one another. Marriage and family life are intended to be of mutual help. The church is to function in a way that renders mutual help to each particular fellowship of believers.

SEVEN AREAS OF ONGOING RENEWAL

As you begin to see more and more of your potential become a reality, you need to subject these seven areas of your life to ongoing renewal.

1. Continually Reaffirm Your Commitment to the Lord.

How would you complete this statement: "Today, in my life, I am most committed to . . ."?

Do you feel committed to a person you love, earning your college degree, caring for an elderly parent, your job, your church, your team, your weight-loss diet, getting out of debt, a political candidate, or a social cause? Have any of those things become your reason for living? To what or to whom are you most committed?

If you completed that sentence with anything other than "Jesus Christ" as your number one commitment in life, I challenge you to reevaluate your priorities.

Now complete this statement: "In my life I am most committed to accomplishing . . ."

Do you deeply desire and feel committed to retiring at age fifity, living until you are a hundred, getting married and raising a family, building a financial portfolio that will fund a relaxing retirement, paying off your mortgage, winning a particular award, or achieving a major career goal?

If you completed that sentence with anything other than "what God created me to do" as your number one commitment goal, I challenge you once again to reevaluate your life.

The direction of your commitment and the depth of your commitment are major factors in the pursuit of your God-given potential. In fact, you will never reach your full potential without focused, deep, and unrelenting commitment. You will pursue what you are committed to with perseverance and enthusiasm, and they are the things you are most likely to accomplish.

I will never tell another person how he or she should live, other than to say, "Follow God's leading about who He made you to be and what He calls you to do." However, I will tell you this about my life commitment:

I am committed to being obedient to God, no matter what.

That is my life statement about commitment.

It covers every aspect of my life. I choose to obey God and leave all the consequences to him. That mind-set puts me into the best possible position to receive a full portion of His guidance, provision, protection, and rewards.

2. *Continually Reaffirm Your Priorities.*

What are my personal priorities?

First, spend time listening to God about what He wants to say to me and what I should preach to the people He has placed before me.

Second, prepare to preach the gospel—which means not only preparing the words to say but also my heart and my mind to deliver God's message.

My goal for any given week starts with, "Come Sunday morning . . ."

When the Lord's Day arrives, I need to be prepared. I need to know that I am doing what God has asked me to do. I need to be bold in delivering what I believe are His words for me to say.

There are many times when I stand in amazement with free-flowing tears at the awesome privilege that God has given to me. I cannot comprehend, and never will, how the Lord could love me as much as He loves me, or how God could entrust me with as much as He has entrusted to me. I have both the joy and the responsibility of delivering a message every week that will reach tens of millions of people around the world. *In Touch* television and radio broadcasts are seen and heard in nearly every nation of the world. They have been translated into more than one hundred languages. Study programs related to these messages are available on the Internet and serve as instruction to millions more. I cannot comprehend the privilege, nor can I lose sight of the fact, that God expects me to succeed at what He has called me to do. I must work diligently to do my best to prepare and deliver the message as clearly and irresistibly as possible, through the power of the Holy Spirit to the glory of God. The results are His. The preparation is mine.

By Sunday evening, I'm already thinking about next week's message. What does God want me to say that will encourage, inspire, instruct, help, teach, guide, and motivate the person sitting directly in front of me next Sunday as well as someone sitting in front of his or her television or computer screen in some far-off place?

To do the work that the Lord has asked me to do, I absolutely must keep my heart clean, my mind clear, and my schedule balanced. I cannot afford any detours or distractions.

3. Reestablish Your Discipline Daily.

Commitment must be coupled with discipline. That means we need to say yes to the right things and no to the wrong things—and do so consistently over time.

Every person is confronted with dozens and dozens of choices every day. Look at your morning routine and you likely will find that you make twenty or more choices before you even get out the door. They will range from whether you have a morning prayer time to what you will wear to whether you will take an umbrella with you. You will find yourself considering what to pack for lunch after you choose what to have for breakfast. You will choose whether to leave the house on time and whether you will read the newspaper, watch the news, or spend time studying your Bible. You will make choices about your day, including when you anticipate coming back home and what you will do that evening. Every one of those choices boils down to simple yes-or-no decisions.

Those daily decisions build the habits you adopt. And those habits determine your overall lifestyle.

The discipline you develop will help you remain consistent in your good habits.

Your discipline and your lifestyle are two primary factors that ultimately forge your character.

No life of integrity, accomplishment, good health, loving relationships, or high value happens without discipline.

Living a disciplined life means sometimes doing things you don't want to or don't enjoy. Life sometimes presents us with tough choices. The disciplined person must say no when it is the appropriate answer and yes when it's the answer God wants to hear.

Most likely, you have not been created or called to do what I have been created and called to do, and vice versa. While God's will, plan, and purpose is different for every individual, He creates and calls each of us to reach our full potential in order to help accomplish and fulfill His greater will, plan, and purpose on this earth. From God's vantage point, there are no fluff roles, no junk positions, no unimportant jobs, and no insignificant goals built into His divine plan. Every gift is established in you for a good and worthy purpose, and the Lord expects you to prepare so He can enable you to succeed.

No matter what God has set before you, resist the temptations to become distracted or take a detour.

4. Reaffirm Your Desire to Do Your Best.

Nobody is perfect—ever, at any time! But I can truthfully say that I have given my best to every sermon I ever preached.

That's all God requires. He takes your effort from there. He has infinite ability to turn your mistakes toward good and to transform your flaws into something fantastic. You can't do it, but He can. Trust Him.

Go to God today and say, "Lord, please help me do my best."

Then get busy. Do what lies ahead of you. Trust God to take your efforts and lead you toward the finish line that He has in mind for you.

5. Rekindle Your Enthusiasm.

There is nothing wrong with ambition. It can be defined as the strong feeling of wanting to succeed in life. Ambition is the desire to achieve something great.

There is something terribly wrong with unbridled ambition, however. Unbridled ambition says, "I will succeed and have what I want, no matter what. I don't care who I hurt or what I destroy in the process, as long as I get what I want."

People with unbridled ambition set their goals and devise their methods totally apart from God and without regard for other people.

On the other hand, genuine godly enthusiasm and motivation go hand in hand. The more enthusiastic you are about the goals God is giving you, the more motivated you will be to pursue them. Stay enthusiastic about your life and your future!

6. Continually Refresh Yourself in the Lord.

Set aside time every day to sit quietly in God's presence. Praise Him. Spend some time reading one or more of the psalms. Thank Him. Talk things over with Him. Listen for the Lord to speak to your heart.

7. Revisit the Vision God Has Given You for Your Life.

Write down the insights God has shared with you about your potential. Review periodically what you have written.

These are seven areas of renewal that you can choose to maintain daily until you reach your final day. Every hour you need to be committed and disciplined. Stay focused on your priorities. Strive to do your best. Stay motivated and refreshed in the Lord. Finally, be keenly aware of the vision God has for your life. You can live in an ongoing state of renewal only if you rely on the Holy Spirit to be your constant and unending source of joy, love, faith, and confidence. Ask Him throughout the day for His insight, His comfort, and His wise counsel.

God wants you to fulfill your potential.

Choose to want what He wants.

CHAPTER 12

THE BEST
IS YET TO COME!

The night that I awakened with the concepts of this book running through my mind and heart, the Lord spoke deep within me these words as I prepared to go back to sleep:

The best is yet to come.

I have absolutely no doubt about the truth and wisdom of those six little words.

No matter who you are . . .

No matter what gifts and talents God has given you, or the degree to which you have developed them . . .

No matter the accomplishments, achievements, or degree of success you have already experienced in life . . .

God still has *more* for you. There's still something to be and do. His very best lies ahead of you.

How can I be so sure of that?

Because if you are in right relationship with God, what eventually lies ahead for you is eternal life in heaven.

You have absolutely no concept of how fantastic heaven is. You may think you know, but anything you know is only a small fraction—if even that—of the way it really is. You have no concept of what it is going to be like to live in the near presence of God and to have an eternity to do all that He might ask you to do. As a person with a finite mind and body, you can't begin to fathom what it will be like to live forever in an unlimited mind and body. You may have experienced great love here on this earth, but it is nothing compared to the depth of love you are going to experience in heaven. The same is true for joy, fulfillment, and every other good thing you can imagine.

Between now and when you go to heaven, God desires to build upon what is and take you from height to greater height, from strength to greater strength, and from glory to greater glory. That is His plan for every believer. Therefore, no matter what you have known as the best of life in the past is only a prelude to the next greater thing that God has for you.

Ask God today what you can do to better prepare yourself for what lies ahead. Ask Him to reveal ways in which you need to pursue your full potential. Ask the Lord to tell you where to make changes that will allow you to receive all the blessings He has in store for you.

Do you need to ask God to cleanse your heart or your mind?

Do you need to ask Him to give you a greater awareness of your natural and ministry-related gifts and talents? Do you need more insight into how to develop what He has already built into you?

Do you need better health—more energy, endurance, or vitality? Ask God to show you what you might do to get and stay physically fit. Also, pray for Him to heal you in areas where you need healing.

Do you need to reevaluate your relationships? Ask the Lord to help you develop ones that are truly helpful and godly.

Do you need to gain God's guidance about how to balance your schedule?

Do you need to summon the courage to take the risk of pursuing a Holy Spirit-inspired opportunity?

Eliminate anything standing in the way of you pursuing your God-given potential with all your heart, soul, mind, and strength. Face up to, deal with, and overcome any obstacles in your path. Ask God to work in you to make the changes you need to make. Believe that God's best lies ahead, and then get ready to receive it.

Don't wait another day to reach your full potential for God.

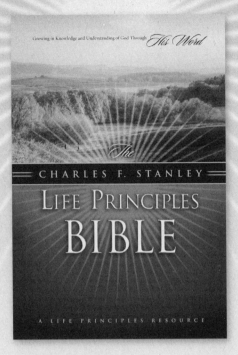

With almost 200,000 in print, THE CHARLES F. STANLEY LIFE PRINCIPLES BIBLE communicates the Life Principles Dr. Stanley has gleaned from the Word through more than 50 years of teaching and pastoral ministry. The result is a Bible overflowing with practical articles, notes, and sidebars that help readers understand what the Scriptures have to say about life's most important questions.

Features include:

- 30 Life Principles with expanded articles
- "Life Lessons"
- "Life Examples" from the people of the Bible
- "Answers to Life's Questions"
- "What the Bible Says" about various topics
- Concordance
- Available in both New King James and New American Standard versions

Other Books by Charles Stanley

The Life Principles Series

STUDY GUIDES